THE
SELF-ESTEEM
TRAP

THE
SELF-ESTEEM TRAP

RAISING CONFIDENT AND COMPASSIONATE KIDS IN AN AGE OF SELF-IMPORTANCE

POLLY YOUNG-EISENDRATH, PhD

LITTLE, BROWN AND COMPANY

New York   Boston   London

Little, Brown and Company
Hachette Book Group USA
237 Park Avenue, New York, NY 10017
Visit our Web site at www.HachetteBookGroupUSA.com

First Edition: September 2008

Little, Brown and Company is a division of Hachette Book Group USA, Inc. The Little, Brown name and logo are trademarks of Hachette Book Group USA, Inc.

Names and some characteristics of individuals portrayed in this book have been changed so that the confidentiality of each is completely protected.

The author gratefully acknowledges Beacon Press, Boston, for granting permission to reprint portions of *Ordinary Time* by Nancy Mairs, copyright © 1993 by Nancy Mairs; Joseph Schachter for granting permission to reprint portions of *Transforming Lives,* edited by Joseph Schachter, copyright © 2005 by Rowman & Littlefield Publishers; and International Creative Management Inc. for granting permission to reprint portions of "Prairie Fire: The Life and Death of a Prodigy" by Eric Konigsberg, originally published in *The New Yorker,* January 16, 2006.

Library of Congress Cataloging-in-Publication Data
Young-Eisendrath, Polly.
　The self-esteem trap : raising confident and compassionate kids in an age of self-importance / Polly Young-Eisendrath. — 1st ed.
　　p.　cm.
Includes bibliographical references.
ISBN-13: 978-0-316-01311-6
ISBN-10: 0-316-01311-0
　1. Self-esteem in children. I. Title.
BF723.S3Y67　2008
155.2 — dc22　　　　　　　　　　　　　　　　　　　　　　2008002224

10　9　8　7　6　5　4　3　2　1

RRD-IN

Printed in the United States of America

For my children, your children, and their children

CONTENTS

THE
SELF-ESTEEM
TRAP

Introduction

I wrote this book because I was at the end of my rope. I had sat hour upon hour in my psychotherapy practice with my heart aching for anxious parents who worried that their teenage and older children lacked good sense and empathy for others, and then more hours with well-educated adults in their twenties and thirties who were already discontent with their desirable lives, and still more hours with young mothers bound to impossible ideals for themselves and their children. One day something in me snapped. "Enough!"

I had read every book out there on idealizing and indulging our children. For all that I read, though, I could not find a foothold that allowed me or my clients to climb out of the box we were trapped in. It felt as if we had glue on the bottom of our feet. The box is our shared cultural attitude: that everyone is special, a winner, with the potential to be great.[1] Inside the box we believe that everyone has something extraordinary to contribute to life and that being ordinary is an embarrassment. This attitude makes a powerful demand on parents and children and creates excessive self-focus and relentless desires to be or have the best. And although parenting experts have critiqued and studied what's inside this box, we have not been able to step out of it. Stepping out is too painful if we blame ourselves personally for being stuck here in the first place, or if we see no other alternative for happiness and self-confidence.

In the 1970s and 1980s teachers and parents began a campaign to cure low self-esteem in our young.[2] Hoping to increase children's creativity and self-expression, this educational and parenting movement unwittingly promoted a self-esteem trap: unrealistic fantasies of achievement, wealth, power, and celebrity. When these expectations are not met in adult life—as inevitably they are not—the result is a negative evaluation of the self. And the trap of negative self-absorption cannot be eased or helped by more focus on the self. Quite a few good books have already been written on this subject, some based on studies and others on clinical observations.[3] They identify a problem, although they call it by different names. And yet no one has uncovered the roots of the problem or found the cure. Obsessive self-focus, restless dissatisfaction, pressures to be exceptional, unreadiness to take on adult responsibilities, feelings of superiority (or inferiority), and excessive fears of being humiliated are the pervasive symptoms of the problem, recognized by those who are trapped and those of us observing them—mental health professionals, educators, parents, and grandparents.

I could use labels like "narcissism" and "entitlement," but I believe they are insulting, especially when used in a judgmental, diagnostic, or accusatory way.[4] Instead of labeling, I want to get us out of this harmful trap and to stop us from blaming ourselves and others. And so I decided to write a book myself. I have written many books and given many public and professional lectures on child and adult development. Writing books helps me understand what I don't understand.

I thought I would be well equipped to write this book. For more than twenty years, I have been a Jungian analyst, a psychologist, and a psychotherapist.[5] Within the broader discipline of psychoanalysis, I am also quite familiar with a specialty called self psychology, which looks at the wounds we accrue from being overly idealized or diminished by our parents. My own research and academic backgrounds are in human development, and I have taught and extensively studied child and adolescent development.

But working on this project has been much harder than I thought it would be. I have encountered acute sensitivities and painful confusions on all sides of the self-esteem trap. First of all, no one wants to be blamed and everyone fears they will be. No parent wants to hear that a cherished child is unhappy because of something the parent has done. Second, parents and grown-up children are in conflict about whether entering adulthood is harder or easier now than in the past. Third, we are only just now coming to understand how long (until the midtwenties) it takes the human brain to mature and thus for young people to master the skills necessary for autonomy—for making sound decisions to guide their lives. Well past those early childhood years when you might believe that development is complete, teenagers and young adults are still developing their identities and values.[6] And finally, everyone gets prickly about the topic of the self. While working on this book, I learned to avoid talking about it at dinner parties. Just mentioning it seemed to make people uneasy. It's as though we all fear that we'll get stuck in the self-esteem trap—becoming easily irritated and overly self-concerned. All of this made it clear that I needed to find the right tone in which to address the problem. A lot of squirming and thought and effort has gone into finding that tone, and I'm sure I haven't always got it right.

So if I sometimes offend you, please forgive me. I want to be honest about what I see as a professional and a human being. I am deeply sympathetic with the suffering on all sides of this problem, especially because I am a parent and grandparent myself. But the stakes are high when we talk about the self.

Soon after I began to write, I realized that I was dealing with a broad cultural issue, not just a psychological problem or a difficulty involving only certain types of parenting or families. In my own experiences as a mother and an educator, I began to sense a shift in our cultural ideals for children sometime in the 1980s, but I wasn't sure how to put my finger on it back then. I wondered if the restlessness, self-obsession, and cynicism that I witnessed in youth and children had to do with the dying out of "traditional" parenting, the kind that I grew up with, where the lines between the generations were clearly drawn and a hierarchy of power was always in place. Many of my colleagues (experts in clinical psychology) claimed this shift was more the result of "attention deficit": youngsters could no longer sit still and pay attention to what was going on because they were conditioned to ever shorter attention spans.[7] Where I saw a lack of manners or respect for elders, others saw a biological disorder or the widespread effects of TV, computer games, popular music, or other aspects of youth culture. I couldn't be sure of anything.

Recently I was happy to find a definitive research study conducted by psychologist Jean M. Twenge that has provided a welcome clarity. Her study conclusively shows that there has been a tectonic cultural shift in what we teach and expect from our children. People whose birthdays fall between the early 1970s and the 2000s—adults now in their thirties down to grade-schoolers and toddlers—have all been marked by this change. In her conclusions from a massive intergenerational study of 1.3 million Americans, Twenge says, "Born after self-focus entered the cultural mainstream, this generation has never known a world that put duty before self."[8] She dubs this generation GenMe. I will use her term—GenMe—throughout this book, grouping under it, just as she does, the age cohorts popularly called Gen X (people born in the late 1960s and 1970s), Gen Y (people born in the 1980s and 1990s), and Millennials (people born in the 2000s).[9] She demonstrates that a central ideology holds these widely different age groups together.

Above all, GenMe'ers have heard that they are unique individuals with talents and strengths of their own: they're "special." GenMe'ers often feel that the "opportunities" supposedly open to them are, in fact, *demands* to be creative and successful in extraordinary ways. While on the surface it may seem that greater advantages should automatically translate into increased self-confidence and autonomy, sadly the opposite often occurs. The trouble with being special is that it promotes a self-esteem trap: excessive self-consciousness, isolation, and relentless self-criticism. The most troubling effect of the trap is the depression and anxiety that come with not being able to "live your dreams."

What does it mean to be or feel special? Literally the word means exceptional, singular, surpassing the usual. "Special" is often confused with its companion, "unique." "Unique" literally means one of a kind. It's a mistake, then, to say that someone is more unique than someone else, because you can't compare one-of-a-kinds. If everyone is unique, that's the end of the story: being unique is ordinary. But when someone says, "You're so special!" that statement carries the implication of standing out, going beyond the usual. In a society like ours, which already emphasizes individuality and competition, the label "special" can become an anvil around your neck, an unnecessary extra weight.

In the 1980s when I first noticed the shift in our cultural

tone, I read a landmark study that has been in the back of my mind while writing this book. Published in 1985, it was entitled *Habits of the Heart: Individualism and Commitment in American Life.* A large-scale, multiauthor sociological review, *Habits* warned us that we might be going off course in our strong emphasis on individualism:

> *We find ourselves not independently of other people and institutions but through them. We never get to the bottom of our selves on our own. We discover who we are face to face and side by side with others in work, love, and learning. All of our activity goes on in relationships, groups, associations, and communities ordered by institutional structures and interpreted by cultural patterns of meaning. Our individualism is itself one such pattern.*[10]

This study is evidence that many scholars were thinking hard about the problem of the special self in the 1980s, even while parents and professionals were promoting it in children. Instead of helping our children learn how to work, love, and share in their families and communities, we taught them to focus on their own achievements and expectations for success. We worried endlessly about their self-esteem. Why?

This book provides the best answer I can give. I offer it in the spirit of dialogue with my readers. I feel I already know the way many of today's parents and young people suffer, and I don't want to add to anyone's misery. Shifting our attitude, I believe, is the key to climbing out of the self-esteem trap and removing the anvil of the special self. Without blaming yourself or others, keep your eye on the fact that we have all been trapped in this box together. The problem of the special self is not the fault of individual parents, children, teens, or adults themselves. It is a mistake made innocently by a whole generation, out of its own need. In the book I trace the roots of the self-esteem trap back to the childhood of Baby Boomers (my own generation). Then I move on to the solution.

I draw throughout on my decades of psychotherapy practice, my knowledge of human development, my personal experience as a parent and human being, and many theories from contemporary psychology. I also draw from various religious traditions, most prominently from Buddhism — of which I have been a practitioner and student since 1971. Buddhism turns upside down our Western psychology of the self and offers a truly fresh point of view that sees our interdependence — our give-and-take with others — as the foundation of self-confidence and happiness. At the core of its teaching about everyday life is the wisdom that we suffer greatly from taking ourselves too seriously and assuming that our own achievements, wealth, power, or celebrity will deliver lasting contentment and meaning.[11] In addition to psychology and religion, my approach here has also been distinctly influenced by the extensive interviewing and research that I've done for this book. From those interviews, especially, I have made some assumptions about you, my reader.

Some Assumptions About You

First, I assume that you are troubled by the self-esteem trap — from your own childhood, as a parent who wants to do the best possible job for your children, as an educator of young people, as an employer or manager who works with young people, or as a therapist who has felt trapped as I did. I mentioned earlier that we all get prickly when we begin to talk about the self. We want to ask, "Whose self?" and "What can you say about me as an individual without knowing me?" Well, I would claim that a portion of our identity is shared and that we help ourselves a great deal by becoming aware of what our culture or society says about what it means to be human and an adult at any given moment in time. The assumptions and expectations for our identity have changed greatly throughout even recent history, and they make a big difference to how we experience ourselves as individuals.

I will talk about this in the book. Here I want only to mention a few other topics that often come up when we talk about self-esteem and being special. For example, from research and experience we know that appearance and achievement often link up with being seen as a special girl.[12] Athletic prowess and power (which can stem from achievement or intellect) link up to being seen as a special boy.[13] In certain ways, we hold different values for what is special when it comes to the genders. While it's useful to understand the ways that gender affects how we evaluate ourselves, it's not a subject that I'll go into here. It has been the topic of several of my earlier books, including the recent *Women and Desire: Beyond Wanting to Be Wanted*.[14] The complexity of gender and specialness would take me too far off the path I want to pursue in developing a new approach to self-confidence in this book.

In a similar vein, social class often comes up in talking about the trouble with being special. Overpromoting and overpraising achievement and success in children has been understood by many experts as being principally a product of middle-class and upper-class parenting.[15] When I began the research for this book, I was thinking along those lines myself. Some people have argued that working-class parents emphasize the boundaries between generations and expect more respect, perhaps even leaving their children at a disadvantage in being assertive or claiming what they want for themselves. In the process of doing my research and writing this book, I have come to the conclusion that we cannot draw strong class-related lines around the self-esteem trap and today's emphasis on being a winner. I believe it affects all kids and adults, no matter their social class, because it sets up a broad frame of reference for identity and values in adult life. Media, schools, and advertising have emphasized the ideals of being exceptional and special in ways that affect all of us in how we think about ourselves.

I want you, my reader, to know that I have thought a lot about your sensitivities, anxieties, and pain in relation to the self-esteem trap. All the same, in order to write a book that you can, I hope, read easily and quickly, I have had to limit my focus. I am quite aware that my approach is not always comprehensive nor specific to everyone's situation. In addition to gender, other topics I haven't addressed here are abuse, neglect, and trauma. If you have encountered any kind of trauma in your growing up or in your adult life, some of my generalities may be off-putting or ill-fitting. I ask for your indulgence. My focus is on one particular, widespread problem: the effects of stressing special talents, individual achievements, and great expectations as if everyone can be extraordinary. In some cases I have overlooked the subtleties of this problem in order to stay as clear as possible about the central themes.

My Research and Interviews

Soon after I began research for this book, I decided that I would not draw principally from my psychotherapy clients for accounts of the self-esteem trap. Because the topic stirs all kinds of sensitivities and self-consciousness, I didn't want to bring my own clients "onstage," even with identities disguised. In the end I have used only a few examples from my own clinical work and just one extended example of a young man in therapy with someone else.

Instead I decided to interview a variety of different kinds of people. I talked with young adults—people in their twenties and thirties now—who have grown up in GenMe. I wanted to hear about their lives and ask them what it was like growing up with a focus on being special. I also talked with educators, school police, social workers, school counselors, and other mental health professionals who work with families, children, teens, and young adults in settings in which the effects of the special self are felt on a daily basis. I asked questions about learning, love, and work and the relationships that are involved. Although I had a general format of questions, I followed the lines of conversation that developed spontaneously between me and my interviewees once we got going. I gave my questions to them in advance, and we went back to the questions if we drifted too far off topic.

I have made use of everything I collected during my year of research, some things quite explicitly, and others as implicit background. The interviews that are included appear in one of two ways. When an interviewee is given only a first name, it is a pseudonym and I have presented the person's story with some level of disguise and have combined it with others' stories. Other interviews appear with the full name—not a pseudonym—and the affiliation of the interviewee. In all cases, the quoted passages are verbatim and have been consented to by the speaker. Besides interviews, I also conducted an anonymous survey of college students at three universities.

Because I live and work in central Vermont, much of my research was conducted in the Northeast. I phoned educators and experts and asked them for names of people I could interview. I also called people whose work I had read or heard about. I asked friends in other places to connect me with experts. I also asked some of my interviewees for their recommendations of others I could contact. Focusing on my surrounding geographical area gave me some unique insights into the self-esteem trap. A lot of the books I read in preparing to write this one were researched in cities or in crowded urban areas where parents and children were driven to have and be the best in terms of material rewards and other outer signs of success (such as getting children into the most elite schools, starting with preschool and ending with Harvard).

In some significant ways, Vermont contrasts with urban settings. Many urban expatriates (like me) have chosen to make Vermont home in order to simplify life, be closer to nature, and remove some of the pressures to identify with materialistic values that abound in American cities and suburbs. Many couples settled here in the 1970s and 1980s to raise their children in a place that would protect their innocence and enhance humanistic values. But as much as I love and embrace the culture of my adopted state (I've been here twelve years), I have discovered a kind of specialness here too: a type of perfectionism about food, exercise, and creativity in family life that can lead to the trap of believing that life can be controlled in order to do everything "just right." Perfectionism is a condition in which our ideals prevent us from being realistic, flexible, and modest. For instance, from the 1970s into the 1990s in Vermont, there was a fairly widespread philosophy that demanded that children be seen as inherently complete individuals who simply needed the right kind of nurture, support, and freedom to unfold into the special selves they were born to be. This way of thinking can also lead to troubles with being special.

In writing this book I have spoken with different kinds of

people from different kinds of settings, of different genders, races, and ages. The self-esteem trap is expressed in many forms and voices. I am sure that you will find a voice that resonates with yours in these pages, no matter your age or where you live. And if you would like to respond to me with your own thoughts or questions about the self-esteem trap, please feel free to visit my Web site at www.young-eisendrath.com and let me know what you think.

Finding a New Center

A certain amount of self-concern and self-focus is necessary for keeping our lives on course, no matter what age we are. But feeling trapped in shame, anxiety, pressure, or competition (even if only in your mind) is a royal road to misery. When you're worried about yourself or feeling humiliated or defective, it's hard to relax and even harder to accept yourself just as you are. The ordinary joys and pleasures of life pass you by, and you may come to feel that you are being cheated of something fundamental, even if your life is going well and you have all the comforts that you need. The trouble with being special is that it frequently leads to being trapped in negative self-absorption.

Parents and children have been taught otherwise: that being and feeling special leads to happiness and positive self-regard. It is deeply and sadly ironic that it has almost the opposite effect. Within these pages, I ask us all to take stock of what we've been feeling in relationship to ourselves and others, and to find a new kind of self-confidence and compassion for ourselves. Grounded in our shared humanity and interdependence, it's something we can call "being ordinary." Gradually, as we grow and develop, we come to recognize that our lives do not belong just to us, to do what we please. Throughout our lives, and especially in childhood, we are sustained and cared for by countless others. Giving back the gifts we've been given—to people and other beings—is the clear path to happiness and self-respect. It might seem counter-intuitive or confusing that being ordinary is a goal that we might aspire to, but it is truly an achievement. Ordinariness is rooted in a wisdom about our human condition and a knowledge of how we are all connected, always making use of one another. Basing our lives on the importance of being ordinary—a member as well as a leader, dependent as well as dependable, and compassionate about the demands that life makes on all of us—is a whole new approach to self-confidence.

CHAPTER ONE

The Trouble with Being Special

Adrienne is a tall, slim, stylish, and attractive thirty-three-year-old woman, a successful psychiatric resident likely to become an excellent psychiatrist. Although she is divorced (without children), she appears from the outside to have her life together. Her peers and colleagues look up to her. She has met her career objectives, presents herself well, and has a very athletic lifestyle that includes biking, hiking, and yoga. She lives in a small, comfortable house with her dog and two cats in a beautiful neighborhood on the north side of Chicago. From the outside, one would guess Adrienne to be confident and relatively happy (except maybe for the divorce).

Not so. Despite her impressive achievements, Adrienne feels trapped in negative feelings about herself and afraid of being alone. Since her divorce, her parents have been supporting her financially. She doesn't really want to grow up, she says, and is uncertain about what direction she wants her life to take. "I mean, how do I deal with the world out there if I'm not getting a grade?"

Good grades were a big part of Adrienne's childhood. Like many high-achieving young women, she grew up in an upper-middle-class household and went to good schools. She was bright and pretty and healthy. Her parents repeatedly told her that she could do anything she wanted, and that she should set her sights high because she was so capable and held so much promise.

The only major difficulty Adrienne faced during her years of living with her parents was an eating disorder, one that developed in the summer after eighth grade. All Adrienne remembers about how it started is that she came home from camp, having had the best time there she had ever had, and her mom said, "It looks like you gained a little weight." Adrienne looked at her hips in the mirror and they looked too big to her. "I was mortified. I remember looking at the other girls and making comparisons, and I just started dieting. And it was extreme. Mostly it was through exercise and competitive swimming. I was about my full height then, around five ten, and I went from 135 to 113 fast."

Adrienne's parents insisted that she see a psychiatrist and that she follow all of his advice and instructions. Although Adrienne strongly resisted the intrusion on her control of eating and exercise, it appeared, at least on the surface, that she cooperated with her therapist. She went on to a good private high school where her mother was on the faculty, did well there, and then was accepted into the elite Ivy League college that she most wanted to attend. In college she did well with her grades and social life. All of these successes culminated in acceptance into the medical school of her choice.

Adrienne has fulfilled many of the dreams that middle-class and upper-middle-class parents have for their children. She has been successful in all of her academic endeavors, got into an Ivy League college and graduate school, is moving into a career that will pay well and be challenging, and has many good friends. And yet Adrienne is far from happy or satisfied with her life. When she thinks back to her youthful expectations, she seems a bit astonished. "My expectations were sort of fantasies. Maybe not even fantasies, because for a fantasy you have to have some kind of image or picture. I just thought that things would fall into place for me. In the last few years, when I realized that my marriage wasn't working, I just freaked out. It wasn't in *the plan* that anything would go wrong for me." When I ask about her goals for her life now, the first thing she says is, "I just want it to be easier." Then she poignantly sums up her thoughts: "I'd like not to sink into this darkness."

Adrienne's unhappiness is typical of the self-esteem trap in many young people in their teens, twenties, and thirties who have received the best care, attention, education, opportunities, and expert help their parents could provide. In my therapy practice I see young people like Adrienne who are confused about their negative self-absorption and restless discontent, afraid of the challenges of living out in the world without their parents' support. Many of them are children of Baby Boom parents. I also see many parents who are themselves distressed at the outcome of their dedicated parenting. Having done their best to give their children everything they could possibly need, these parents are hurt, baffled, disappointed, angry, and fearful about their children.

I meet with Marie, a woman in her forties, in weekly psychotherapy. Marie works as a school counselor and exudes a warm, motherly attitude that telegraphs her Italian American roots. She started therapy with me because of power struggles and communication problems in her marriage to Andy, her husband of twenty years. Although Marie primarily needs to lighten the load of the emotional baggage she's brought from her childhood into her marriage, she now spends at least half of every session worrying about one or the other of her two teenage children.

On one particular occasion she was crying, and then even sobbing, as she told me about an emergency she had experienced a few nights before. At home with her nineteen-year-old son, Michael, she had had a gallbladder attack and was in terrible pain. Sweating heavily and barely able to speak, she called out to her son to bring her the telephone. He seemed shocked when he saw his mother and asked curtly, "What's wrong with *you?*" She answered that she was very ill and might need to go to the hospital. He replied, "Could you hand me the phone when you're done? I'm in the middle of ordering a pizza."

As I sat and listened to Marie, I realized that I was reacting as a mother as well as a therapist, a fellow traveler on the seemingly impossible road to raising a responsible, alert, compassionate young adult. My heart went out to Marie, knowing how hard it is to be the parent of a teenage child.

As a mother and grandmother to some terrific and responsible young people, I have made it a personal mantra to say "There's no way to get it right" when it comes to being a parent, and "If you muddle through and everyone survives, then you've done a good job." On one hand, I am immensely proud of all my progeny. On the other hand, everything I say here about the struggles of being a parent applies to me as well. My children also have been troubled by the self-esteem trap, just as Adrienne and Michael have. Their lives have been shaped in part by a style of parenting and educating that has dominated child rearing for the past several decades—a style that continues. In fact it is being embraced by new parents, who are locked into a cycle of cultural demands and effects they might not even be aware of, in danger of enlarging upon the mistakes of their own parents. As a parent and as a therapist, I believe that never before has it been so confusing and destabilizing to be a parent. And never before have we had a generation of such confused and unhappy young adults whose lives seem desirable from the outside. Something has gone drastically wrong.

The Problem

America's children are suffering from a particularly threatening and perplexing problem. Obsessive self-focus, restless dissatisfaction, pressures to be exceptional, unreadiness to take on adult responsibilities, feelings of superiority (or inferiority), and excessive fears of being humiliated are the pervasive symptoms of the self-esteem trap, as I mentioned earlier. Even in very young children, we can witness the beginning of these symptoms—for instance, when a child seems unable to step back from her own needs when they are in conflict with another's more important needs, such as Marie reported with her teenage son Michael. The self-esteem trap, in its least troubling form, leads to unhappy adult children who feel defective because they are unable to have or be what they imagined for themselves. At its worst, unchecked over childhood and young adulthood, and reinforced by other social conditions, it can lead to chronic emotional disorders such as depression, narcissism, and addiction.[1]

Jason, a young man in his early twenties, came to see me in therapy because he had a distinct feeling that he was superior to others. He didn't like the feeling. He didn't know how he had gotten it, but it made him uncomfortable socially. When Jason met new people, at first he was interested and enthusiastic about getting to know them. But then within a month or so, he would notice himself judging them. He would quickly and gleefully identify their flaws and weaknesses. Eventually he would find himself to be superior, better, or more capable than others who had initially intrigued him. He felt a pressure to succeed, to be better than others, almost all the time. He was uncomfortable around, and uninterested in, those whom he secretly found lacking, yet he felt ashamed of his incessant judgments. This whole range of thoughts and feelings was terribly upsetting to him on many different levels.

Jason is stuck in the self-esteem trap. The special self demands that its owner constantly measure up to extraordinary standards, try to win every competition, and fulfill a specific or vague grand fantasy about what the self and its life should be. As this young man sensed, this identity becomes a prison, an eternal trap from which the person feels there is no escape and no chance of rescue. After all, who else is capable of rescuing you if you're better than everyone else? The special self is a lonely and scary place to live.

The most threatening aspect of cultivating this kind of self is its hair trigger for feelings of humiliation and shame. When the person fails, even for a moment, to meet the demands of this self—to be the best, the thinnest, the smartest, the most witty and most successful—there is a plunge into a kind of black hole, the darkness that Adrienne referred to. It feels internally like dropping or falling through the floor into a dark space where one is all alone and cannot be helped. The higher the pedestal, or accomplishment, or fantasy, the harder the fall.

Most frightening is the feeling of being all alone, which comes from an inability to believe in any reliable context or group or community that will sustain the self. This all-aloneness makes it difficult to feel empathy for others (except for close friends who seem to have the same problems and views) and further encourages a negative preoccupation with the self. Ironically, although by definition the special self feels like a personal problem to each individual who suffers from it, it is ubiquitous among today's youth.

When I listen to people like Adrienne and Jason in psychotherapy, it strikes me immediately how unrealistic their expectations are. Believing from an early age that they are exceptional, even extraordinary, they often don't accept older people as role models. They also reject the milestones or road markers that signal that they are just beginners on the career or parental path, that all accomplishments are a process, and that they have a long way to go before they are expert.[2] Being a beginner feels humiliating. Being ordinary won't do. And this unwillingness to feel ordinary, flawed, less than perfect, can be traced back to how they were parented.

Because caring parents are quick to blame themselves for the suffering and unhappiness of their children, I want to be very clear here. This is not a book about blame. The self-esteem trap is complex and rooted in many cultural causes, and it is *not* the intentional doing of any devoted parent or child. Understanding it allows us to become responsible for changing our approach and to support one another in the process. My decision to write this book came directly from my heartfelt sympathy and sadness for dedicated contemporary parents, and for restless, unhappy young adults who have come to me for help. We're all trapped in the belief that everyone is great and a winner, deserving extraordinary opportunities to become an exceptional individual. Getting out of this trap requires finding a new kind of self-confidence and compassion for ourselves. Grounded in our fundamental shared humanity and interdependence, as I said earlier, this new confidence is rooted in being and feeling ordinary. Feeling ordinary comes from a wisdom about our human condition and a knowledge of how we are all connected. In the 1980s we were duly warned by the social researchers who wrote *Habits of the*

Heart that the human self can never truly be independent of a network or community of people; but we very much lost track of that idea when we began to emphasize being special. What happened?

To answer that question, we will first analyze some contemporary parenting practices in order to see how they affect children's chances of becoming confident, responsible, and compassionate adults. We will also look from the inside and the outside at a range of troubling developmental experiences of children who have had caring, dedicated parents. We'll meet people like Adrienne, Michael, and Jason, who are old enough to serve as examples of the outcomes of parenting practices that stress that each child is a winner. Today's families are raising our future. And many of them are in trouble.

The World Out There

All of our efforts to be good parents take place within a social setting that is bigger than our families and friends. Social climates affect what we take to be the truth about everything we do. In recent decades, as I've been saying, parents have been told by experts that they should boost their children's self-esteem by praising them often and noting their unique and exceptional talents. We are also in a climate of biological reasoning about how children grow up.[3] Even though you may know next to nothing about the science of genetics and proteins, you probably subscribe to the idea that some of your children's behaviors come from inherited tendencies.[4]

When parents come to see me for psychotherapy, they look back to their memories of Aunt Millie or Grandpa Jones to explain at least some of their children's strengths and weaknesses. Little Anna is hyperactive because there's a lot of manic-depression in her genes. Adam has ADD (attention deficit disorder), just like his father, but Adam is getting medical treatment for it and hopefully won't fail in school as his father did. Sixteen-year-old Sarah seems rather depressed lately and talks a lot about hating herself, but that's probably due to PMS (premenstrual syndrome), which her mother and sister also suffer from.

Parents often come with these explanations even if they know little about the scientific validity of this way of thinking. They don't question these ideas because their doctors, neighbors, children's teachers and counselors, and friends subscribe to them. In other words, biological reasoning about their children's difficulties is supported by the social climate. Parents, and their young adult children, also hold on to these ideas because they can *do something* about the problems (get a diagnosis, get medications, make special academic arrangements), and these ideas do not further burden parents with blame laid on top of what is already a load of self-blame. Conscientious parents tend to blame themselves first these days and then look to others to blame, usually not their children.

In this book I will not offer many biological explanations, although I will talk about some of the findings of neuroscience that can help us understand how the self forms and develops in a growing child. I will not fight with these kinds of explanations either, although to be frank I believe they are harmfully overused.[5] Instead I want to take the larger view of how we've been raising our children since the Baby Boom generation grew up and became parents themselves.

Being the Center of Attention

As I've said, obsessive self-focus, restless dissatisfaction, pressures to be exceptional, unreadiness to take on adult responsibilities, feelings of superiority (or inferiority), and excessive fears of being humiliated are the symptoms of the self-esteem trap in young adults, and sometimes even in children or teenagers. Linked to these kinds of complaints are predictable struggles that I witness in dedicated parents. Both in therapeutic and in social encounters, I see conscientious parents who are unintentionally held hostage emotionally by their children—toddlers, elementary- and middle-school children, and teenage or older children. Parents seem to be in charge of their infants, but even there vast amounts of attention and engagement can be given over to every gesture of a baby. From toddlerhood on, many children hold the apparent advantage of control in social situations. When children repeatedly scream, demand, threaten, lie, fail, require special arrangements and material things, and fall short of taking on their age-appropriate responsibilities, they are in an awkward position of premature social power.

Undoubtedly you have witnessed or been a part of this kind of power struggle.[6] You're dining in a restaurant or in someone's home and a toddler, a grade-schooler, or a teenager is dominating the scene. The small child may be interrupting or running around. The parents may be embarrassed, sheepish, or indulging, but they cannot get the child out of the center of attention. The school-age child may be asked by adults to give opinions or facts that demonstrate the child's knowledge or prowess. Some young children simply join in any conversation, feeling sure their opinions are welcome. A teenager is more likely to dominate the social scene by sulking and disengaging when asked what he wants to eat or do. In these moments when children are dominating, adults usually feel uncomfortable but are unwilling to express disgruntlement or criticism because they fear they would be seen as intolerably callous or rude. After all, these are children. Shouldn't the world revolve around them?

No. When you're a child, assuming or counting on being the center of attention can lead to distorted relationships and identities that undermine later confidence in fitting into a network of people, knowing the give-and-take of community, and recognizing that adversity and process are built into accomplishing anything in the adult world. No more than fifty years ago, a child-dominated social scene like this would have been unimaginable. Although children might be present and even acting badly from time to time, they never presumed to be equal to adults in their social ranking.

Most of us have been annoyed by these symptoms of being special in children and parents. So with all of the good books and persuasive studies on this topic that already exist, as well as the awkward social situations and confusion and unhappiness of our adult children, why does this problem still persist? Because for the past two decades caring parents have been told that teaching their children they are special will produce good self-esteem and lasting happiness.

Self and Self-Esteem: A Brief History

To understand how this came about, we need to start at the beginning, with the self. The human experience of a self-conscious self is unique in this world, although it's likely that other animals have a rudimentary sense of self.[7] Maybe you don't think much about what your self is most of the time, but if you're a parent, you've probably given a lot of thought to the self-esteem of your child.

The self is the experience we have of being an individual contained in this bag of skin we call a body. Human beings everywhere, no matter their culture or society, have this sense of being separate little units with personal histories and unique identities.

Even in societies whose languages have no or few personal pronouns (like "I," "me," "mine"), there are words that mean "the action comes from here" or "the action comes from over there."[8] All societies hold adults responsible for their own actions to some important degree. Our society holds young people to be accountable for themselves at the age of twenty-one. In the past this meant that young people needed to feel ready to assume full financial, legal, and psychological responsibility around the time of their twenty-first birthday. Many people married and had families in their young twenties.

The word "self" refers to what we experience on the inside—our personal identity, our sense of being in a body, our ability to act for ourselves, and our personal story. We use the word "person" to refer to what we see from the outside, the solid, three-dimensional object that moves and acts like a human being. I think of the self as a function of a person, something like the beating of the heart or the circulating of blood. The self function is active and would be better expressed as a verb than a noun. Expressing it as a noun misleads us into believing it is a thing; often we come to identify the self with our body, the most solid thing about us. And yet when you think about it even a little, you know the self is a function you need in order to be a person, but it is not the same thing as being a person.

At the beginning of the twentieth century, many important European and American values and ideals culminated in the belief that there was enormous promise and power in the individual. The idea of individual genius—most often illustrated by Einstein, Darwin, and Freud—became very central to the new field of psychology that was just beginning, having developed primarily from philosophy. The psychoanalyst Carl Jung, who, with Sigmund Freud, was a founder of psychoanalysis, was especially interested in the self—particularly its individual creativity and uniqueness. He believed that the best of our humanity was expressed through our individuality.[9] He also believed that our individuality carried its own unique imprint or stamp, built in from the beginning. Just as each acorn grows up to be an oak tree and not a maple, Jung believed, each self had its own form, meaning, or purpose. He dubbed the gradual unfoldment of that purpose "individuation." Individuation could be delayed or disrupted by early family problems, trauma, or abuse, but it was understood to have its own natural force or organization. If there was an obstacle to the unfoldment or force of individuation, from emotional or other disruptions, then effective psychotherapy could remove the obstacle and restore the process of becoming a unique individual. As a Jungian analyst myself, I am quite familiar with this theory that there is an inherent blueprint for creativity or self-expression in each of us that sets us apart from all others.

Jung was not alone in his emphasis on individuation. Many of the early developmental psychologists, clinical psychologists, and psychoanalysts felt that the self was like a seed that grew on its own if a child was nurtured, disciplined, and understood in the right ways.[10] But this focus on the self turned out to have within it a serious error that has only recently been corrected by new discoveries and theories of human development.

By the end of the twentieth century, psychologists, philosophers, linguists, and sociologists reshaped the theory of self, emphasizing its interdependence. Experts now claim that the primary unit of human development is a relationship—initially a dyad—not an individual.[11] After all, we humans come into being as a couple (a mother and child), and we are throughout our lives dependent on others in order to know ourselves and express our talents and abilities, as well as fulfill our needs. The notion of individual genius has given way to the idea that all creative work and leadership take place within relationships and community. Until an adult is able to share and collaborate, to give and take, he will not be capable of expressing and sustaining ambitions and talents, not to mention family and relationships. This relational theory does not discount the importance of individual talent, insight, or hard work, but it puts these into perspective: people need others in order to bring about anything worthwhile. Our accomplishments will always depend on emotionally intelligent relationships with others. Even the self—the experience of having an identity and a story over time—exists only in relationship to others. The self is what we rehearse of what others say about us; what we react to in what others do to and with us; and what we see in how others mirror us back to ourselves.

In the twenty-first century, then, what's important about the self? First, we all need the functions that it provides: the feeling of being in our bodies, the knowledge that we are responsible for our actions and speech, the story of ourselves over time, and the attachment bonds that come with the self and keep it alive. These self functions support our autonomy—our ability to make sound decisions for ourselves throughout our lives. But they can be disrupted, or can develop poorly or out of balance and be distorted, especially through the relationships we have with others, first with our parents and siblings. So the second important thing about the self is that it is always dependent on relationships. Living happily with ourselves as adults means having a reliable give-and-take with others who surround us and who support and sustain us and our worth.

What about self-esteem, then? What is it, and why does it get so much attention? Most people think that self-esteem means feeling good about yourself, but this contemporary dictionary definition is more accurate: "An attitude of acceptance, approval, and respect toward oneself, manifested by personal recognition of one's abilities and achievements and an acknowledgment and acceptance of one's limitations." [12] So your self-esteem includes knowing and accepting *both* your strengths and your weaknesses. You discover your strengths and weaknesses from the effects of your actions in the world (what you do and produce) and how others see you, reporting back to you what your influence has been on them. Good self-esteem comes from actual accomplishments and relationships; it is the by-product of doing some things well, accepting your limitations (when you need help from others), and seeing the good consequences of your own influences.

Self-esteem can never be simply implanted by others' comments, but it can be interfered with by too much criticism or too much unearned praise. Today's parents tend to offer too much approval and enthusiasm for their children's very existence, disrupting the child's growing ability to discern the truth about her own effects and actions. [13] Effusively praising every step she takes, every task she completes, every soccer play she executes, and every book she reads fosters the self-esteem trap. If nothing is expected as an ordinary part of becoming a civilized member of a human group, then a child may come to feel important for breathing—a belief that will not serve him well. One frustrated grandmother recently told me, "I was shocked when my daughter celebrated her son's toilet training. Having a party because he could poop in the pot! Man, I thought, we are really in trouble here. This kid thinks he's done something special in becoming civilized. But this isn't an accomplishment! It's just part of life!"

When caring parents ooh and aah over every small effort, and especially when they praise either ordinary or mediocre accomplishments, children become confused about the realistic assessment of their actions. Should they believe what Mom or Dad is saying, or should they look further at just what is going on? It takes a lot of time and development in order to refine that guiding inner voice at the axis of your being, that voice of true self-esteem and self-compassion that will give you reasonably good feedback—realistic and humane—about your effects on others, your abilities and flaws. Over time, children can actually lose confidence in their own capacity to assess themselves if their parents overpraise, and this leaves them (teens especially) very susceptible to peer pressure and pop culture.

When the "special self" was first created, about a hundred years ago, people thought it would be the key to happiness and authenticity. But ironically, some of its most lasting results are negative self-absorption, an undervaluing of being ordinary, and difficulties with seeing ourselves accurately and compassionately. Our late-twentieth-century cultural focus on everyone being a winner has led to an epidemic of exaggerated, and usually negative, self-consciousness in children and youth. Not only is this epidemic expressed in the self-esteem trap, it's also obvious in awkward and uncomfortable social situations in which children seem to be in charge, and it leads to the kinds of unhappiness and suffering that Jason feels in his twenties and Adrienne in her thirties. Although both are smart and well educated, they're afraid of the slings and arrows of fate because they lack realistic self-esteem and confidence in being ordinary. As I've said, a major symptom of the self-esteem trap is a hair trigger for shame or humiliation for ordinary human failings, mistakes, and less-than-perfect beauty, success, and achievement.

Perhaps worse than anything else is the self-hatred that ensues from failing to meet the great expectations of being special. Overfocus on the talents, skills, or insights of an individual child (no matter how gifted) naturally leads to an exaggerated self-importance in adolescence and young adulthood, and then getting a warm pizza may automatically block out the ability to listen to an ill mother.[14]

Our children become preoccupied with their own needs before they have any chance to develop that inner voice of self-esteem and self-compassion that accurately assesses their strengths and weaknesses and allows them to appreciate others with a spirit of gratitude and generosity. Accurate self-esteem includes a knowledge of our weaknesses and limitations. It allows us to acknowledge when we need the help of others, as well as what we can do independently and well. In learning about giving and needing help, children increase their good feelings about themselves as they come to see that everyone struggles (it's not personal) and everyone can help. Even a preschooler can learn to be attentive to others' feelings and concerns, especially to the adults who are providing sustenance and resources. And it's not just that feeling special produces too much self-absorption. Rather the trouble with being special is that it prevents an openness to feeling ordinary and discovering a fundamental wisdom about our human condition: the knowledge of how we are all connected, always making use of one another to respond to the normal adversities of human life.

A New Kind of Self-Confidence

This book draws on many sources to overcome the self-esteem trap, but there are two traditions that I emphasize: Buddhism and psychoanalytic psychology.[15] Although Buddhism can be called a religion, it is not practiced in an exclusive way. Its methods can be followed by anyone—a member of any other religion or of none at all. So I will be sharing some Buddhist teachings with you that can open our eyes to a new way of developing.

In contrast to the Western emphasis on the importance of an

individual self, the long tradition of Buddhism offers a path to self-confidence that is based on a skillful engagement with our interdependence. Interdependence is the web of relationships that sustains us moment to moment in support and inspiration. Teaching collaboration and sharing as the basis for self-confidence provides parents and children myriad ways to develop and learn to help one another. I'll describe many of these throughout the book.

On the other hand, I have recognized a critical lesson from psychoanalytic psychology that I do not find well defined in Buddhism: that our autonomy is essential to our development, beginning in childhood and continuing throughout life. Autonomy is not the opposite of interdependence but, when done well, its enhancement. Through our autonomy we become self-governing, capable of guiding ourselves by our own decisions.[16] This is a skill that has been stressed in Western psychology and philosophy because our enlightenment movements (philosophical, social, political) have promoted and protected individual freedom—the right to make decisions for ourselves. Our Western focus on individual freedom has at times been distorted by the assumption that the individual is a unit unto herself or himself, as I have said. But many Asian cultures, with their deeply ingrained caste systems and hierarchies of race and gender, have underestimated the importance of self-determination in human development. Psychoanalysis and psychology help us to understand how making choices and dealing directly with their consequences teach us about ourselves and the world that we inhabit.

Robust self-confidence, self-determination, self-compassion, and resilience are founded on learning early and repeatedly that true happiness comes principally in two ways: being able to relate to others in a caring and kind manner (since we always depend on others, we need to sustain our connection to them), and knowing how to be responsible for ourselves and our actions. With these two as their foundation, children will have the best preparation for a life of creativity and self-confidence, instead of restlessness and negative self-absorption.

I want to introduce one more fundamental teaching from Buddhism here, because it bears directly on the problem of negative self-absorption: human life always includes discontent and adversity.[17] Whoever you are, bad things will happen to you, no matter how hard you try to keep them away. It's not a personal problem of yours that you meet up with obstacles and failures. Human beings do not have a lot of control over their lives, even though they have responsibility for their actions and decisions. Because things inevitably fail to go as we'd like—and besides, we all get ill eventually and die—we must learn how to respond realistically and compassionately to pain, loss, and difficulty. Being ordinary, we recognize that we cannot escape difficulty but we can learn from it. Learning from difficulty and loss becomes the basis of a fundamental wisdom about transforming our suffering into insight and compassion for ourselves and others.

In a recent issue of the *New York Times Magazine,* a lengthy article was devoted to scientific research that is now being done on wisdom in several university settings in America and other countries. One passage particularly caught my eye:

> *Where does wisdom come from, and how does one acquire it? Surprisingly, a good deal of evidence, both anecdotal and empirical, suggests that the seeds of wisdom are planted earlier in life—certainly earlier than old age, often earlier than middle age and possibly even earlier than young adulthood. And there are strong hints that wisdom is associated with an earlier exposure to adversity or failure.[18]*

Adversity can strengthen us and even open doors to our sense of purpose and deeper happiness in helping others.[19] And so we need repeatedly to acknowledge to ourselves that dissatisfaction is a part of life. No one escapes it, and no amount of material things or status can protect us from it. The sooner children learn this, the easier it is for them to accept that failures, stresses, and losses are to be expected—and not to blame themselves or others for them.

If children mistakenly believe that their own accomplishments or possessions or status will make them happy and sustain their lives, when these things do not deliver the wished-for outcomes, they (whether growing or grown) will assume that the self is the problem. They will fall into the self-esteem trap: regarding themselves as defective (not smart, pretty, talented, fast, or clever enough) and turning a hatred toward themselves, exaggerating their undesirable qualities and diminishing their positive characteristics.

Caring and dedicated parents have unintentionally left their children open to this trap of humiliation and despair about themselves. We'll discover, though, that there are many ways for young adults to climb out of this trap, and for parents with children of any age to redirect themselves and their children toward a new kind of self-confidence, rooted in being ordinary, interdependent, and autonomous. In order to do this with our eyes open, we have to see what went wrong, and why, when the Baby Boom generation became parents.

CHAPTER TWO

The Roots of the Problem

Mention the phrase "Baby Boomers" to anyone under the age of fifty and you're likely to be met with glazed eyes. The idea of listening to, and learning from, the past generation—especially parents—is not a popular one. And yet if we cannot see what happened before we embarked on life's path, we are likely to remain confused and unrealistic about our current situation. For many GenMe'ers, though, even rebelling against a parent seems passé. Feeling on a par with their elders, convinced of the lasting value of their own youth culture, teens and young adults of GenMe often perceive their elders as simply irrelevant. Many are dubious about seeking direction from elders on anything but the most mundane issues, because they didn't look up to their parents and now they cannot trust or respect anyone who is part of their parents' generation. This disconnect results in a tendency to erase traditional social protocol at work and at school.

One fifty-five-year-old supervisor told me about his newly hired administrative assistant, a thirty-year-old woman. During the first week of her job she e-mailed him, writing, "OK, so I've scheduled your meeting for Wednesday at 10 AM and I would suggest you invite the following people for this one. . . ." This young woman fully believed she was doing her job well and hoped to be rewarded for her ideas. She was completely unaware that her tone was disrespectful.

Professors on college campuses across the country are dealing with the same issue.[1] One told me of a new college advisee who skipped his first scheduled meeting, instead leaving a voice mail from the ski slopes. "Hey, dude! This is Ron, and you're my adviser. I need to get into this course, can you do that for me?" This professor, an accomplished man in his sixties, explained that his graduate students never call him Dr. or Professor anymore. He has come to expect to be on a first-name basis with students, even when they introduce him to their children.

When I think back to my own adolescence, I recall how strict my parents were, and how I rebelled against their authority. But I didn't abandon the hope of being guided by someone in their generation. Although Jerry Rubin warned, "Don't trust anyone over thirty," like many in my generation, I wanted to be guided by elders I admired. And in fact I always showed outward respect for my parents and believed that the sacrifices they made for me deserved honor, whether or not I agreed with their beliefs and methods.

It seemed to me back then that I had a "natural" feeling of modesty about myself and never overstepped it with any elder, unless I was specifically invited to do so. Now I see that this feeling was not natural, but was trained into me. I didn't worry about navigating the social hierarchy because I knew how to respect those beyond my rank. I had had to respect all of my elders in childhood, and this training served me well in making my way up the social ladder to gain privileges, increase my possibilities, and find support from many generous mentors—especially because I was an ambitious woman at a time when female ambitions were very much discouraged.

But when it came to raising my own children, I did not demand that they respect me or others in my generation. I felt, strangely enough, that I should *earn* my children's respect instead of expect it.

A Boomer Childhood

I grew up in a working-class world. My entire childhood took place in the same homogeneous environment—small one-floor, two-bedroom houses, street upon street, that were inhabited by families that mostly seemed just like mine. Fathers went to work at local factories in the early morning hours and came home in time to have supper, somewhere around 5 PM. They were tired and grumpy at dinner and might be irritable or sleepy afterward. They spent little "quality time" with their offspring, except on weekends. Some fathers drank, at bars on the way home or after dinner. Mine did not.

My mother was the hub of the family wheel, as most mothers were. Whereas my father came from a ragtag American family (some parts hillbilly, some parts Native American, and some parts outlaw), she came from a Slovenian family that fashioned itself as an ethnic tribe. My mother looked down on my father and his family. She was the boss inside the house and ran our home like a well-oiled machine or a factory. My home life was similar to that of other first- or second-generation American families; we followed the rules of the Old Country. Everything had a place, and everything was in its place.

My mother told me how to do everything. Her major rule was "cleanliness is next to godliness," and I was to behave according to that rule. Every day had a schedule and a theme: Monday was laundry, Tuesday was ironing, and so on, until Sunday was church and rest. Everything was predictable and orderly.

I had many chores and jobs, my schoolwork being the least of them. Although I performed very well in school, my parents had little interest in my grades. I dutifully brought home my report card, which always had straight A's, and put it on the kitchen table. Both of my parents voiced worries about my getting these perfect grades. My father would say things like "I hope you're not getting a big head. And, you know, your teachers don't know everything." My mother would say I should loosen up and "learn to toss a ball around sometimes." Chores at home were always considered more important than my schoolwork.

Both of my parents believed in proper training in everything from vegetable gardening to floor scrubbing. Each chore I did was inspected and critiqued. I was also expected to earn money to donate to the family income, starting at around the age of twelve. Because there were few babysitting jobs available where we lived, I took in ironing and did lawn work in the neighborhood in my early teen years. My training included being spanked (usually by my mother in a hesitant, ceremonial, but serious way) when I did something really wrong, and being screamed at and denied privileges if I sassed my parents or expressed my opinions when they were not specifically asked for.

My parents also taught me about right and wrong, and made sure that I memorized and understood the Ten Commandments. Indeed I was extremely anxious about performing well in the eyes of God, whom I thought was watching my every action. On a scale from one to ten on scrupulosity, I would have ranked ten-plus. I was the type of child who pondered the woes and wrongs of the world and did not want to enlarge either. This being so, I was not always the most popular kid, but I had plenty of friends I could count on. I could also count on the shared conscience of my friends, who were raised with the Ten Commandments or the Golden Rule in mind. If circumstances warranted it, though, my friends and I made allowances for life's difficulties. When one of my best friends in high school suddenly became a compulsive liar after her mother died, we cut her a lot of slack. We could see that she was coping with grief and shame, even though we didn't know the words. We guessed that her lying had something to do with trying to make herself feel better.

In my childhood and adolescence, everyone I knew went to church or synagogue and stood by the social and ethical norms of religion. My parents, devoutly religious and very simple folk, often explained the miseries of the world with a philosophical attitude: "There, but for the grace of God, go I," or "God gives and God takes away." I felt comforted by this philosophy. Being part of the working class, we were surrounded by families who struggled even more than we did to make ends meet. I considered myself lucky because I always had enough food and respectable clothes. My parents also donated a certain amount of their small income to charity and acted very generously toward anyone who came to our door needing help. They insisted that I be generous in giving away a part of my allowance as well.

Although these routines and structures may sound harsh, I experienced them as wholly fair and predictable. The emotional problems I faced while growing up were not from parental demands made on me, but from the fighting my parents did with each other. My parents argued openly and even brutally, although I did not witness any physical violence between them. I was often very afraid during their fights: afraid that they might harm each other, not me. My aunt and uncle, who lived next door, did fight physically, and so I knew firsthand that women could be beaten by their husbands. My sympathies were always with my mother in the conflicts I witnessed between my parents.

I was expected to be my mother's companion, confidante,

and friend. By a stroke of fate, rued by her, I was her only child. When I was in elementary school, she confided to me that she did not like my father. She demanded all the same that I show respect for him. Neither she nor my father seemed to know how to be friends with each other. Each hoped to be friends with me. My father clearly felt he had lost my friendship because of my mother's open complaints and judgments against him. He tried unsuccessfully from time to time to talk with me. I recognize now that my loyal sympathy for my mother was due largely to the fact that I knew her story better than my father's. And I believed her line that she did "all the work around here," although my father was the sole breadwinner. She did not honor his strenuous labors, apart from the backhanded compliment that he didn't "drink or run around with women, squandering his paycheck," the way some men did.

In my youngest years, my special closeness with my mother seemed to provide a heavenly softness among the demands of life. Each day we had some time together, just the two of us. She taught me many board games and played them with me. When I studied at home, she wanted to learn what I was learning, and we would talk about what I was studying. She had had to leave school at the age of thirteen and spoke longingly about wanting to continue her schooling (although she never did). As I gained knowledge beyond what she had, I would tutor her. For a time, this was fun. From middle adolescence on, though, her emotional needs seemed more and more burdensome, as I gradually felt (though could not have said so) that she envied and belittled my achievements.

When it came time to leave home, I couldn't wait to get out. The world beckoned to me; I had read about it, but I had not seen much beyond my neighborhood and school. My high school years had included holding down a twenty-hour-a-week job as a telephone operator, leading several school organizations, and being valedictorian in a class of four hundred. I credited my success to hard work, not innate intelligence. I did not feel I was owed anything by the world unless I earned it. I felt quite confident I could work my way through what the world might demand of me. I had already proven I could work hard, earn a good income, and pursue my own interests and studies at the same time. And most important, I knew that my mind and my life belonged to me. I never for a moment imagined that my grades, my interests, or my motivations for the future were the concern of my parents or anyone else. This was a tremendous, although bittersweet, freedom, since despite my autonomy I very much wanted my parents' happiness and approval for my achievements.

My childhood certainly had its distinctive features, and my parents may have been stricter than most. And yet I have written about it at length because I believe it had some important similarities with the majority of Boomer childhoods. These crucial features led us, as a generation, to long for praise and approval. This longing was so strong that it blinded us to many beneficial components of our growing up, and the role they played in our later successes. Parental authority, coping with adversity, the discipline of daily life, moral and ethical training, and an emphasis on contributing to the welfare of others were largely forgotten when we became parents ourselves.

The Search for Self-Esteem

As a generation, why were Boomers so hungry for positive self-regard that they overlooked many important lessons from their own childhoods? To answer this question, we need to step back and think about the social context in which Boomers grew up.

The Great Depression and World War II left the parents of

Boomers preoccupied, afraid, and dedicated to making the world a better place and to raising families that could survive, no matter what. The ongoing threat from the Cold War was palpable in the air-raid drills and bomb shelters that were expected to protect them in case of a World War III. Many fathers had known firsthand the trauma and misery of war and the devastation it could bring. The background of economic vulnerability and the memories and threat of war shadowed fathers especially, making them emotionally unavailable, distracted, and ruminative. Other unique conditions also affected families in ways that were different from previous generations.

First, families tended to be organized into nuclear units, separated and cut off from extended members.[2] Like my neighborhood, communities were homogeneous and either upwardly mobile, wanting to be upwardly mobile, or suffering from not being so. The post–World War II period was one of economic opportunity and the expansion of the middle class, and fathers wanted to take full advantage of advancing their careers and families. Consequently they were away during most waking hours, not just up the street or across the meadow (as they might have been before automobiles dominated daily travel), but miles away.

The women who had worked in factories during the war were told to go home now and do their new jobs of being mothers exclusively. They were to become experts in Homemaking, something that their own mothers had simply performed but not named or celebrated. Mothers were cut off from social supports, trapped in small households where they would compare themselves to the fantasy of Betty Crocker rather than to the realities of their own mothers. They were constantly made to feel they didn't have other choices in life, primarily because of their economic dependence. Earlier generations of mothers learned about child rearing and running a household from their own mothers or older sisters (who would have lived nearby). By contrast, these mothers were expected to learn from experts like Dr. Spock, who were not close by to witness their struggles or comfort them.

The nuclear family system, with its rootlessness, also put new pressure on couples to have a marital "romance" or some kind of intimate companionship between them. With no skills and no models for this, both men and women felt like shameful failures in their marriages. They blamed each other. My parents knew nothing about how to be friends with the opposite sex, and they fought incessantly because their family backgrounds were so different and because my mother expected a lot from my father that he could not deliver. They were like warring tribes. I know, from thousands of hours of doing couples therapy, that many other families had a similar Cold War atmosphere at home every day.

All this took a toll on the emotional lives of mothers and fathers, but it was the mothers who were home, needing to talk or simply feeling trapped in their own unhappiness. The strength of Boomers' personal daily exposure to their mothers' psychological needs—especially their anger, guilt, shame, and depression—was unique in the history of American families. In earlier eras, mothers had their own mothers, sisters, and brothers available to them for emotional support and childcare. Until the post–World War II parenting generation, even new mothers could return to work on the farm or in the family business, with extended family available for childcare. Middle-class and upper-class women would pay for childcare and felt no guilt about leaving their children with wet nurses and nannies, even for lengthy holidays. Our foremothers had resources and possibilities for themselves that postwar mothers lacked.

Children everywhere will always try hard to meet their parents' emotional needs.[3] Children hope against hope for happy, healthy parents to care for them. If parents are not happy, children will do their best to provide, challenge, and cajole them into it. If that doesn't work, children will just make up an illusion of an adequate parent to stand in place of a truly inadequate one. Trapped with a deeply unhappy or angry mother, children will try to behave, entertain, advise, escape into fantasy, or—when all else seems to fail—become the problem child to distract the mother's attention.

The powerful emotional needs of mothers, the long absences and fatigue of fathers, and the abuse Boomers might have suffered at the hands of their parents meant that they grew up in the Them Generation. Their lives were about Them. They—mothers, fathers, older siblings—dominated the emotional space. Most important, Boomers confused feeling loved by Them with meeting *their* emotional needs. When they met the needs of their mothers, as I did when I sat for hours reading to and tutoring my mother, children could feel close, connected, and warmly received, possibilities that otherwise were usually not available. In these circumstances, most Boomers were known and loved for filling the role of daughter or son, not for being unique individuals with their own needs and capacities.

I have repeatedly asked myself what it is about the Boomers that made being seen and known as individuals so pivotal. Previous generations of children were no doubt ignored, demeaned, and abused at least as much as Boomers were. I now believe that the mobility and isolation of the nuclear family played an important role in their plight. These conditions thrust mothers into social and emotional turmoil and robbed children of a grandmother, grandfather, or uncle who could have recognized the individual worth of a developing child. In the generations before the Boom, children were often known as individuals by extended family members who were not as busy with daily life responsibilities as parents were. And in these earlier generations, the work performed by children on the farm or in the family business might have been more visible and real than the work Boomer children did, lending a sense of personal worth, such as I felt in earning money working outside of my family. The principal job of Boomer children was to keep their mothers happy. This job could never be rewarded by either parent; it wasn't legitimate work.

When I look back to my own childhood, I know now that I hungered for the attention I got from teachers and other mentors because it contrasted with the kind of attention I got from my mother. Although my mother responded warmly when I paid attention to her, she was not interested in knowing more about *me;* she was interested in my knowing more about *her*. I find this is a common occurrence among Boomers. I believe we came to feel guilty and ashamed of our own needs and desires in a way that other generations did not.

When Boomers left home at the end of childhood, they left with a vengeance that other generations didn't have before and haven't had since. We wanted out, to be completely on our own. Our rapid and final departure from home was, I believe, an expression of not wanting to live for Them anymore. Although we couldn't have said it, we wanted to be noticed as important and worthwhile for being ourselves. Unfortunately this has meant that Boomers have been repeatedly dubbed the Me Generation.[4] This accusation points to the symptom instead of the roots of the problem. We were not seeking the spotlight for ourselves alone, but were trying to discover if we could feel good about ourselves *and* be close to others at the same time. This had not been possible in our childhood.

Boomers created a generational therapy to cure themselves—beginning with the cultural movement for peace, love, and understanding (that only later became sex, drugs, and rock 'n' roll). We gathered in groups large (rock concerts) and small (consciousness-raising) to bring to ourselves the peace and love that we collectively longed for. Eventually we dubbed our problem low self-esteem and started many therapies and movements to help us feel better about ourselves. But this was not the I'm Okay revolution; it was the I'm Okay–You're Okay revolution, as pointed out in the title of a bestselling pop psychology book of the time.[5] We were focused on others' feelings as much as our own.

Finally, when we Boomers became parents ourselves, we cast all of our anxieties about self-esteem and self-confidence into child-rearing strategies that imitated our own cures. We wanted to affirm our children's individual selves and help them grow up naturally, opening like flowers in the sunshine of our positive regard. We mistakenly believed they would thrive if they just got plenty of praise, acceptance, and respect for their own thoughts and feelings. We didn't see this as indulging them, but simply as supporting them.

Unfortunately children are not flowers. We misunderstood self-esteem and self-confidence. They do not come from liking yourself or being praised just for being. They are by-products of doing things well, developing an attitude of self-respect through recognizing your actual strengths and weaknesses, knowing how to be ordinary, and learning the rules and benefits of interdependence, including how to fit into a hierarchy as a beginner and how to learn from elders. Unknowingly Boomers designed child-rearing practices that left their children with the symptoms of being special, instead of a solid foundation for self-confidence and good self-esteem.

Reacting against the Them Generation of their childhood,

Boomers founded a cultural movement that was aimed, unconsciously, at correcting the emotional imbalance from their early family life. Understandably they wanted a win-win setup in their relationships; they espoused an I'm Okay–You're Okay orientation to disputes and conflicts that stressed mutuality, reciprocity, and equality in order to enhance dialogue in all aspects of conflict. This strategy emphasizes the importance of both parties feeling respected as equals. Unfortunately the I'm Okay–You're Okay formula does not work as well in parenting as it does in friendship and marriage.

I'm Okay–You're Okay Parenting

Among contemporary parents (whether Boomer parents of older children or post-Boomer parents of younger children) there's now a continuum of I'm Okay–You're Okay parenting styles: laissez-faire, helicopter, and role reversal. All three have in common the belief that parents and children are on nearly equal footing when it comes to rights and needs, that parents should be friends with their children, and that children's self-esteem must be promoted and protected at all costs. But the styles of the three types differ.

Laissez-Faire Parenting

In this type of parenting, parents are indirect, nonconfrontational, vague, and friendly in their attempts to be authorities.[6] These kinds of parents, often Boomers, don't feel they have much of a parenting style because they don't fancy themselves as authority figures. They generally don't give much advice, or they give advice and then apologize for having done so. However, they want to provide all the best encouragement and opportunity for their progeny, and they love to show off their children's accomplishments and successes. They will usually find some way to undermine or disagree with criticisms of their children by authorities, such as school officials or others outside the family. Laissez-faire parents are laid-back or inconsistent in their discipline, and they try always to see their children in a positive light.

When I asked Adrienne about her parents' authority, she looked perplexed at first, as though my question was strange. Then she answered, "Everything was put back onto my mother when it came to authority." How did her mother convey authority? Adrienne hesitated and then said, "I never recall having her talk to me directly about anything, except maybe about how to do schoolwork, like taking notes. Or she would talk about my girlfriends and stuff." Adrienne's mother also indirectly communicated her authority by telling her daughter about things that happened at the private high school where she taught. From these conversations, Adrienne could glean something about how her mother conducted herself.

Adrienne now believes her parents were confused about how to reach her, especially after her eating disorder started. She thinks they were afraid to impose any limits on her because she would just lose more weight to get the power back. "I had way too much control. If they messed with me, I would just hurt myself more, which also hurt them."

Adrienne's parents were friendly and available, but not directive or authoritative. Laissez-faire parents don't act as authorities unless their children ask for advice, and even then they may be reluctant. I can recall my husband and me saying things like "Well, we're the parents here, right? You're supposed to listen to us, right?" on occasions when we should have cracked down on back talk or arrogance from our teenage children.

Tim Guilbault is a plainclothes school policeman. A stocky but athletic middle-aged guy with a crewcut and goatee, he never wears a uniform at work, but he exudes a clear sense of authority. The kids respect him once they see he will not accept excuses for irresponsible behavior. Until they know this, they certainly test him.

Tim believes that too many parents have become laissez-faire. "The biggest problem we face is that parents run a bunch of excuses for their kids' behaviors. The majority of the time, I hear 'That teacher has it in for my kid,' or 'It's just what kids do at this age.' It's not a hundred percent of the time, but it's probably in the high eighties," he says.

Tim points out that all too often adults want to be friends with children, not authority figures. "We even have teachers here who refer to the students as their friends. This is what I call the I'm Okay–You're Okay syndrome," complains Tim (without any clue from me about my theory of I'm Okay–You're Okay parenting). Tim is especially critical of time-out discipline because, he says, kids do not learn anything about why they are being punished in a time-out. "They have time-out, no consequences. As parents, as educators, we have to fill the role of being authorities and mentors, not friends."

Helicopter Parenting

This style of parenting describes parents who hover around their children and want to be close friends (not just friendly) with them.[7] Rooted in the belief that children and parents *always* need to have pleasant, cozy feelings, helicopter parenting focuses on children's success and creativity, as well as nonconflictual relating. It's most often practiced by post-Boomer parents and gives the impression, to an observer, that the parent is appealing to the child for approval and/or to be the parent's *closest* friend. Unpleasant feelings and negative judgments are avoided. Many younger helicopter parents believe they are experts in attachment parenting and other theories of emotional closeness.

Psychiatrist Dan Kindlon writes about this style in his excellent book *Too Much of a Good Thing,* about overindulging our children. "Compared to earlier generations," he says, "we are emotionally closer to our kids, they confide in us more, we have more fun with them, and we know more about the science of child development. But we are too indulgent. We give our kids too much and demand too little of them."[8]

Helicopter parents unrealistically want little Jonah to be happy 24/7, although they may know that's impossible. If, for example, Jonah wants a costly iPod for his birthday, it's hard for his parents to say no and simply stick with it, even though they believe that buying such an expensive gift for a young child is wrong. When Jonah cries and screams, they worry that he'll feel bad about himself if he doesn't get one, because "all of his friends have iPods." Helicopter parents don't want Jonah to feel uncomfortable, or to have to tolerate too many negative emotions. At times of difficulty, when they could teach the valuable lesson to their son that they are confident he can handle disappointment and limitation, they sidestep conflict and avoid the bad feelings that come with it. They are unwittingly depriving Jonah of the ordinary bits of adversity that will inoculate him against later life stresses. Since Jonah was a baby, they've tried to move the storm clouds away from him. Deep down, helicopter parents may feel anxious or guilty that they don't maintain parental authority and that they want to be friends, but they believe that harshness can crush a child's spirit.

However, they want Jonah to be ambitious and to get into the best possible college so that he has every chance of success.

Instead of helping him deal with reality, though, they minimize his problematic behaviors and are outraged if school authorities punish him too harshly for, say, a "minor" offense like plagiarizing. They will spend hard-earned money to be sure he has all of the opportunities for self-expression and achievement open to him. They overpraise his effort and tend to overestimate his talents and abilities, often putting him on a par with them, his parents. Helicopter parents are also likely to be phoning teachers or school counselors, arguing about a low grade that Jonah "didn't deserve because he put so much effort into writing that paper." In her useful book about contemporary mothering, *Perfect Madness,* Judith Warner describes helicopter parenting: "We make sure that our children's needs are honored wherever they go; they must have *their* foods, *their* routines, unchanged. We teach them that their interests must always be served. And served first." [9] Helicopter parenting sets up a child to be out of tune with social hierarchy and interdependence, and off-kilter in regard to the limitations that must be accepted in order to have good self-esteem.

This style of parenting produces the preschoolers you can see on playgrounds every day, screaming and sometimes kicking at their mothers because the crusts aren't cut off their bread, or because their juice box, while the right flavor, is the wrong brand. Helicopter parents are unknowingly cultivating little tyrants who will, in their teenage and later years, become intensely afraid of humiliation or even depressed when they are unable to be famous or rich or powerful.

Role-Reversal Parenting

The final version of I'm Okay–You're Okay parenting is what I've dubbed the role-reversal style. It's even more mutual, indulgent, and child-oriented than helicopter parenting. It's the full expression of the children-as-flowers fantasy: if you just give children the right nourishment, open affection, a lot of freedom, and encourage their inner genius, they will flourish.

The most extreme variant of role-reversal parenting is a New Age theory called Indigo Children, as described in a popular book, *The Indigo Children: The New Kids Have Arrived*, by Lee Carroll and Jan Tober.[10] The book is a collection of essays that suggest a new breed of children have been born in recent decades. These children not only possess extraordinary intelligence and other creative gifts; they also have supernatural intuition and insight. While they are often obstreperous and difficult to manage, it is because they are ahead of everyone else, including their parents and any other adults in charge. They are spiritually gifted and able to intuit others' emotions. They only want to do the most altruistic things but are hampered by ordinary rules and the inability of adults around them to "get" what they are about. Parents and teachers who espouse this theory believe that Indigo children should lead the adults, not the other way around. The Indigo Evolution, as this movement is called, is a role reversal of the parent-child relationship when Boomers were kids.[11] Where Boomers had to serve the emotional needs of their parents, the parents of Indigos have to serve their children on a broad spectrum of emotional needs for stimulation, opportunity, and power.

Other examples of role-reversal parenting are less extreme but still have the children-as-leaders theme. In an interview about the effects of this kind of parenting on a small-town central Vermont school, I talked with Dr. Andy Pomerantz, now the chief psychiatrist at a veterans hospital. Before he retrained to be a psychiatrist, Andy was the town doctor, the local family physician in his village of Chelsea. His graying beard, slim build, and kind manner are exemplary of a middle-aged Boomer who has devoted himself to helping others and being an active member of his community.

About a decade ago, role-reversal parenting transformed the K–12 Chelsea School, which Andy's three children all attended. The school became entirely child-centered, an environment where adult interference was considered a very bad thing. "There was a word that the administration used," Andy recalled. "It was 'adultism.' Adultism was forbidden at the school. Young people should not be limited in their freedom to explore and develop their creativity. That was the ideal the school was following. There was this belief that this is what you need for creativity to flower. Among other things, kids were coming to school dressed any way they wanted to, half-naked in the warm weather. There was nobody to hit the gong when anyone stepped over the boundaries, if there were boundaries. There was an arrest in the gym because a student claimed that she was raped by another student. It turned out that the kids could have sexual adventures in the gym, right there during school hours."

This public school, supported by many role-reversal parents, was idealistic, nonmaterialistic, and not excessively success-oriented. No one was necessarily trying to get the school's graduates into the most elite colleges. Its aim was more to encourage creativity and spontaneity in the children, permitting them to "become themselves." Even with the most idealistic aims, as we'll see, this style of parenting produces the same problems as the laissez-faire style does: an overestimation of what the world will bring you.

Moving On

Boomer and post-Boomer parenting styles make the mistake of attempting to equalize rank and power between adults and children, sometimes even assuming that children should be in the

lead. I'm Okay–You're Okay parenting focuses too much attention and too many resources on the individual self of children
without cultivating the awareness and skills that children need
to adapt to the hierarchy of the world, to become autonomous,
to be active members of groups and engage in give-and-take
within a community. Ironically and sadly, I'm Okay–You're
Okay parenting deprives growing children of many essential
benefits that Boomers received from their own parents. And yet
any attempt to return to the past and rely on traditional parental
styles will not rectify the situation we now face. Earlier styles of
parenting did not account for the centrality of relationship in
human development, specifically teaching children to develop
emotional intelligence and empathy with others. Nor did earlier
styles have available the scientific information that we now have
about how the brain develops and what kinds of challenges children need to master at each new stage of development. While
traditional parenting did prepare children for autonomy by requiring various chores and duties and insisting that children deal
with their own mistakes or failures, that style of parenting did
not include a critical recognition of the ingredients of autonomy
and how it keeps on developing throughout the life span.

The style of parenting that I am advocating — based on interdependence and autonomy — depends on a "We" rather than a
"Me" or "They" philosophy, but moves away from equality
between parents and children and toward parents as leaders.
My approach also focuses on the importance of adversity, the
necessity of conscience and virtue, the subtleties of self-governance, and the value of being ordinary. I'll also address the role
played by religion and spirituality in our lives and the lives of
our children, as well as how we come to a deep and true love
that can sustain family relationships and friendships over a lifetime. In the end we will examine happiness — what it is and is

not—and how it can be cultivated through a new kind of self-confidence.

And for those readers who are now teens and young adults and who've been deprived of the opportunity to build this kind of self-confidence from the ground up (though your eyes may have glazed over from reading about a Boomer childhood), I'll point the way to a renewal of your own development, through integrating the forgotten strengths of the past.

CHAPTER THREE

The Importance of Adversity

Self-confidence is an essential ingredient for a responsible and satisfying life and helps you to steer clear of the self-esteem trap. It means that you trust yourself and feel assured that you can handle whatever comes up, that you know what to do in the face of challenge. This kind of confidence grows primarily through overcoming adversity, by which I mean circumstances or events that oppose your desires, wishes, or ideals—things that happen to you or problems that you face. Self-confidence grows through experience as we come to know what our strengths and weaknesses actually are. Although realistic praise and encouragement from parents and elders can help to bolster our confidence, it cannot supply it.

As we saw in the last chapter, I gained enormous self-confidence through finding that I could earn an income, study, have a social life, and meet my own goals while I was still a teenager, living at home with my parents. Early trust in myself was built on meeting the many demands made on me. As you read about the description of my childhood, you may have felt my parents were too strict, that I must have been traumatized from their constant fighting, that I was at a disadvantage because I was a working-class girl, and that I probably suffered from stress because I was overscheduled in my later teenage years. Your observations would be accurate. But the difficulties I faced while I was still young, though they left some psychological scars, prepared me well for a fulfilling adult life. With the help of psychotherapy and a number of generous mentors, I have achieved my most important dreams: extensive higher education, earning an income from work I love, having close family relationships, finding a solid footing in the educated middle class for my family and myself, and engaging in a rich and rewarding spiritual life. I even feel a gratitude now for the difficulties of my childhood, because they led to a process of discovery and showed me early that I could count on my own strengths.

Overcoming Difficulties

If you want to feel self-confident, you have to face and overcome difficulties. In so doing you will learn how to work with yourself and others, and you will develop empathy and compassion for human suffering—a priceless insight.

During my telephone interview with Jeannie Norris, the head of Miss Hall's School for Girls, in Pittsfield, Massachusetts, I felt an immediate bond of agreement about problem solving as a means of growth in young people.[1] Miss Hall's enrolls 190 girls, from thirteen to eighteen years old, who come from diverse economic and cultural backgrounds. Most of the girls board, but some commute. "Having raised two daughters and been in all-girls education since 1977, I can say that there is not too much about adolescent girls that surprises me anymore," Norris quips.

She has written about the link between happiness and self-reliance in teenagers. "There's this great search to make our children happy, but parents have not seen clearly that happiness is connected to self-sufficiency," Norris said near the beginning of our conversation. "We have over problem-solved for our children. We rush in and sweep up the gravel on life's road and eliminate any opportunity for our children to work through difficulty and come out on the other side, knowing they have solved a problem and can do it again."

In my interviews with educators and school counselors, the major complaint I hear is that parents "run excuses" for their children, as the school policeman Tim Guilbault put it. This phenomenon of intrusive parental problem solving is a major component of helicopter parenting, as I mentioned in the last chapter. Helicopter parents are well known for speaking on the cell phone several times a day to their college-age and older children. They nitpick the details of their children's challenges and problems. Although parents (and children) may believe that "going to bat" for a child is a virtue, it is harmfully overdone by helicopter parents when it deprives growing children of opportunities to learn from adversity.

One college professor told me a story about an experienced and respected associate dean who regularly advised students about their courses. This man was talking with a senior about some of his courses when the student pulled out his cell phone and said, "Dad, this guy thinks I should take this course. What do *you* think?" The same professor also told me about parents who want to sit in on their college students' career-counseling sessions.

Of course helicopter parents are caring and well intentioned. They assume that their interventions protect their children and will produce young adults who are better informed and prepared to jump into the demands of a responsible life. That's not the case. Excessive parental problem solving actually prevents children from having real experiences of decision making, failing, and cleaning up their own messes.[2] They are robbed of an important foundation for self-confidence and self-respect: coping with adversity and solving the ordinary problems of life. The children of helicopter parents feel as lost and fearful as Adrienne, especially when they separate from their parents and try to guide themselves by their own decisions.

Erik Thompson, president of the Vermont Center for Family Studies and a psychologist and family leadership consultant, has a lot to say about today's parents running excuses for their children. He calls it "running interference." "When we see our children through the lens of anxiety, we make our biggest mistakes of trying to correct the wrongs of our own childhood. That just misses what's going on; it's a transfer of a problem. If I see my kid as weak, then I get the idea I have to strengthen him, but whatever decisions I make about how to do that, I'm making those decisions from my own anxiety and my feeling that my kid is weak."

If instead we allow children to handle their own problems, we get around this transfer of anxiety. It's baffling when parents have no confidence in their children's ability to solve their own problems yet want them to become self-confident. Thompson makes the analogy of strengthening your leg muscles by running. If parents run too much interference in problem solving for their children while the children sit back and do nothing, the parents will get stronger, but the children get weaker and fall over when they try to run on their own.

In 2000 I gave a presentation on my book *Women and Desire* at a conference in Dublin, Ireland. I was speaking to a group of about a hundred mental health professionals and regular moms, people who wanted to know what was useful and what was not in the struggles between mothers and their children.

A lively discussion was under way when a woman—probably in her fifties—stood up and said, "Why should we trust an American to advise us about our children? You Americans don't ask anything of your children, even of your teenagers, and then you expect them suddenly to become adults when they leave home. Here in Ireland we expect a lot more from our children than you do. We expect them to take on serious responsibilities in their teenage years." I agreed with her and thanked her for the comment.

I knew even then that we American parents had a troubling blind spot and that we were paying for it in our children's delaying of adulthood.[3] But I couldn't yet see the bigger picture of what was wrong. Thompson's comments about how we weaken our children by running interference, always trying to protect them from life's difficulties and their own vulnerabilities or limitations, crystallized the problem for me.

Ironically Erik Thompson himself is an example of delayed adulthood. A youthful late-thirties man with bright blue eyes, he smiled ruefully when I asked him if he was a parent himself. "Well, I'm a parent to young children, and most of my friends have young kids. We're all in our late thirties. I think it reflects poorly on us as a society that a lot of educated adults don't choose to become parents until the last possible moment. We are not producing educated young people who are ready to be parents at twenty-five, when my father became a parent. I really didn't become responsible at the level that my father was at twenty-five until I was thirty-five. Through my twenties, I was looking to build up my self-esteem, but now I see that the only way to build self-esteem is by solving difficult problems." I believe that Adrienne, Jason, and other young adults like them would say they do not feel ready to be full-fledged adults. They feel uncertain about how to operate on their own.

Jeannie Norris very much agrees with Erik Thompson and offers another analogy for rectifying the problem of parental overinvolvement. "Think of your child standing to your right and the problem she needs to solve is on your left. If you step between her and the problem, *you become the problem*. She cannot see around you and she cannot see the solution. Get out of the way."

Many caring parents have wondered why their children fight with them so much about problems that the children are having. Repeatedly I've heard parents of teenagers say, "When I try to talk with my kid about the struggles he's having with his friends, he fights with *me* and defends himself. I just want to say, 'Hey, how did I become the problem here?' "

Children will develop an attitude of defensiveness around parents when their parents stand between the child and a problem like failing, getting into trouble with authority figures, or having difficulties with friends. Later, when these children become young adults, they don't feel confident that they can handle what is demanded of them and can easily fall into the self-esteem trap. As young adults not yet knowledgeable about life, they'll tend to feel a combination of idealism—believing the world should meet their demands and values—and cynicism—feeling they've "seen it all." This self-defeating combination comes from having been overprotected and overpraised, as well as from exposure to the "virtual realities" of media, which can seem to substitute for life experience. Helicopter parents too frequently become the misdirected focus of the growing child's angst and anger, deflecting the child's attention from the actual effects of his or her actions and leading to a confusing fog of uncertainty and unreality in dealing with problems.

I often see an unwillingness in today's parents to let the chips fall when their children get into trouble. Take the problem of DUIs (driving under the influence).[4] More often than not, by the time I hear in therapy about a teenage child getting picked up for a DUI, my client (the parent) has already checked with his lawyer to see what can be done to get around the charges, especially if the charges are harsh or seem unfair. It's been my experience that if the charges are softened or dropped with parental intervention, the child gets another DUI. Although I want to be sympathetic with the parent, I also find myself silently saying, "Duh!" The child has not really encountered the consequences of his actions, and so what has he learned? That his parent can run interference, that's all. Even though a teenager may sound remorseful and say, "I'm sorry," or "I know I made a mistake," unless he actually goes through the experience of being charged and having to pay the fine (from his own earnings) or do the penalty, he won't learn from the difficulties he has created.

As a parent myself, I know how tempting it is to offer excuses for younger children: "But the charge was unfair," or "His teacher has something against boys. She really doesn't see how bored he is and how his acting up is an expression of that." What these excuses fail to recognize is that negative feedback is an occasion for a great deal of learning. First, it is an opportunity for, say, an elementary-school child to respond to an authority figure, even though the authority figure may be wrong. Later in life, that child will surely be faced by many other authorities who are even more flawed and problematic than the current ones. When it comes to a fight with authority (other than an indulgent parent), every responsible adult knows that such a fight has to be chosen carefully, because a lot of energy can be wasted on fighting about trivial issues. How do we discover what is trivial and what is not? By going through a number of fights and seeing how things turn out. A child may want to begin fighting authority in nursery or elementary school, and if so, parents should let him fight. He will learn from it. Again, if parents jump in and try to save him from trouble, they will become the problem. Even for preschool children, experiences of adversity — where life falls short of their ideals and wishes — teach them about their own strengths and limitations. Such experiences defeat unrealistic fantasies of being able to remain perfectly in control of what life delivers. Today's children and young adults do not learn those lessons because their I'm Okay–You're Okay parents won't let them.

Some young adults, like Jason for instance, feel they were extraordinarily good and smart in childhood, never causing anyone a real problem. Inevitably, in looking back they see themselves as some version of "perfect" or "almost perfect." If I ask them how they were disciplined or what their parents got angry about, they say, "There was nothing to complain about. I did everything that was expected of me, and even more. I just never got into trouble or made anything but the smallest mistakes."

Erin has this feeling about herself as a child. She is twenty-five years old now — an attractive, somewhat shy, slim blond woman with a very congenial manner. Although she was overjoyed to get into her graduate program and anticipated enjoying her studies, she is not happy. She does not get along with her mentor and is unsure about whether she wants to continue, what she would want to do instead, and whether she even wants to reside on the East Coast. Erin grew up on the West Coast and reflects on her childhood as ideal. "I just grew up and things were very, very smooth all the way through high school. I never had any adolescent angst or anything like that. It was pretty much a golden type of development." After she graduated from college, things changed. Erin agreed to be interviewed because she felt her real-world life, encountered after graduation, was "overwhelming and daunting," and she couldn't understand why she lacked self-confidence about facing her future. "I think the model I had been operating on was that you should already know. Like in growing up, things were pretty structured and clear. You could just perform and do the tasks people told you to do. Suddenly you're faced with really making your own choices, and you have some subtle expectation that you should be an expert already."

After she graduated from college, one of her first jobs was helping out on a sailboat for six months. She didn't like the way she was treated. "I just had a different idea of what my role would be. I thought the learning process would occur much faster or that it would be more like school. That you'd go there and there'd be set agendas and you'd acquire the proper skills to get the tasks done." Instead everything was ambiguous "with what was going on with people and equipment on the boat. I wasn't in a position of power, and I had to depend on other people to guide me properly." Erin had a mild emotional breakdown and fell into the self-esteem trap. "None of my traditional asking questions and wanting to be quickly competent worked, and the discrepancy between what I thought or imagined and what was reality was impossible. It made me hesitant to even want to try new things."

Arriving at the university for graduate school, Erin believed things would be different and her expectations would be met. But Erin did not find her graduate mentor to be as available or helpful as she thought a mentor should be. Eventually Erin dropped her mentor and tried to find a different one in another area of the graduate department. She hasn't found anyone who seems a good fit with what she wants, and she's very distressed and frustrated now.

Not yet even fully out in the world—after all, transitional work and graduate school are still somewhat sheltered environments—Erin already feels confused and uncertain about her attitudes and standards. Legally an adult, she often feels emotionally more like a child, unable to deal effectively with the little bumps of life, not having yet encountered the rugged, bone-jarring shocks that adult life eventually delivers to all of us.

Erin's parents were laissez-faire: very supportive, physically present, but not as authorities. "Mom and Dad were really supportive at home so that my brother and I could spend lots of time and energy in other arenas. My personal needs were pretty much taken care of, so I was able to excel in other settings."

Erin's parents did not overpraise either of their two children. "That's because we really had such high standards that they didn't want to increase the pressure on us. We didn't talk about realistic life paths, though. I was trying to think if we ever talked about family or getting married or having kids. Our home environment was good, but we didn't have any conversations about how life progresses or how you make choices."

Erin claims she never got into trouble in childhood, by misbehaving or performing poorly in school. As I mentioned above, this has to be an idealized memory, because all of us get into trouble. There are frustrations, conflicts, and disappointments on an everyday basis in the real world. If you don't recall *any* from childhood, then it's likely that someone protected you from them.

Learning to Swim in the Rough Waters of Reality

Life presents us all with challenges and conflicts on a daily basis. Caring parents unintentionally weaken their children's ability to deal with the necessary suffering of life when they run interference excessively. This doesn't mean parents should throw their children to the wolves, but rather they should be sure that their children learn how to fight the wolves for themselves before leaving home.

Jeannie Norris sent me some of the materials she distributes to parents of students at Miss Hall's. I find these guidelines to be wise advice for parents of children in elementary school, middle school, and older—even parents of young adults. I have summarized them and modified them for my purposes.

• *Parents need to show confidence in their children and their abilities to deal with the world as it presents itself.* Life is a series of repeated adjustments to change. Children benefit from knowing their parents believe they can make the necessary adjustments that arise from a child's ordinary circumstances.

• *Children should not be allowed simply to transfer their negative emotions to their parents.* If a child is feeling angry, frustrated, lonely, or sad, it's not useful for either parent or child if the child just unloads the emotions onto a parent. When this happens, the child walks away free of worries and frustrations and the parent ends up feeling miserable. When a child is upset, a parent can certainly comfort the child, while keeping an emphasis on the feelings themselves—for example, "I know you feel bad now, but I'm sure you'll be able to get through this."

• *Parents need to teach middle-school and older children basic life skills such as self-care, organization, money management, time management, and anything else that seems like life wisdom, while staying away from solving the specific problems a child is facing.* Instead of saying what a child should do in a problem situation, the parent should say something like "I can see you're upset. What do you think is a good first step here?" It's most effective not to deprive a child of the lessons that problem solving teaches, and so a parent should keep separate the teaching of life wisdom from problem solving for a child.

• *Parents always need to remember to cheer from the sidelines rather than to claim possession of their child's success.* When a child is successful in overcoming adversity or achieving a sought-after goal, parents should applaud from the sidelines and continue to encourage independence in problem solving. Parents have years of experience beyond childhood. If they act as a partner in problem solving and take credit for the success, they can too easily rob the child of the feeling of triumph.

Jeannie Norris talks about today's young people being "information rich and experience poor." This is true for young adults like Erin, who have an abundance of information at their fingertips but lack real-world experience that tests their mettle. Norris makes a comparison between today's young people and the Boomer generation: "We were experience rich and information poor. We were in school to find out what adults knew, but that's not the case anymore. Everyone has access to all kinds of information on the Internet, and these teens have grown up in a time where life experience has been at a low ebb. They have not spent as much time in real life as in virtual living. They think they know about things because they've seen or heard them on the media, but they don't have real experience."

Adrienne and Erin are caught in the self-esteem trap. Though well educated, they are afraid of failing, of not being able to overcome difficulty, and of succumbing to the slings and arrows of fate. Commenting on her experience in graduate school, Erin says, "It's been hard. I thought I would be getting a lot of mentoring and shaping up about how to do research and be a professor, but that wasn't the way my mentor saw it. I've been trying to find other mentors. I thought I could ask for help and just get it, but that's not the case, and now I don't know what to do." Facing serious questions about her future, Erin feels a lot of pressure to make the "right decision." She didn't have the benefit of the kind of parenting Norris recommends and must find a way to jump into adult problem solving, knowing there's no safety net anymore.

Erin needs to try something in which she really risks failing in order to learn that she will cope no matter what decision she makes. When I speak with young people like Erin in therapy, I tell them there are no "right decisions," only actual decisions and commitments. Problem solving in real life never carries any guarantee of being "right." We cannot know if we have chosen the right partner or the right career before making a commitment—or ever, in some cases. Whether we fail or succeed or something in between, we have to make our best judgment at a given moment and then commit to a choice. Whatever the outcome, we will learn about our strengths and weaknesses and how they bring us into relationship with peers or elders in solving problems. Adjustments can be made as long as we know how to work with our negative feelings of shame, humiliation, disappointment—without turning them against ourselves.

You may remember a story from Greek mythology about a boy named Icarus, who was the son of a celebrated architect named Daedalus. Icarus helped his father to make wings of wax and feathers to escape a labyrinth where they were prisoners.

His father, a remarkable artist and inventor, warned young Icarus not to fly too low, where the mist from earth might weigh down his wings, or too high, where the sun could melt them. Off the ground, at first Icarus stayed close to his father, but soon he was enamored of flying and soared high toward the sun. His wings melted, and he plunged into the sea and drowned.

Now you may be saying, "Well, that never should have happened! His father should have carried him along on his back to keep him safe." I have a different solution, one that I learned from my friend Dan Jacobs, a Freudian analyst and psychiatrist. At a conference on myth and metaphor, I heard Jacobs give a talk on this story. He had an original perspective on the metaphor of high flying as inflated self-regard: "His problem wasn't that he flew too high, it was that he didn't know how to swim!" Exactly. If you fly high, make sure you learn to navigate those dark waters—humiliation, disappointment, anger, and depression—when you fall.

If a person believes he is or should be special, he'll tend to apply the brakes when he encounters challenges that might bring him down. If he believes or has been told that he's the best, the wittiest, the fastest, or the funniest, he'll be petrified of failing. Since there is always the possibility of failing at something he hasn't done before, he'll avoid diving into new or rough waters. If he assumes he's the only person he can really trust, then he'll try to think through all potential problems in his own head before he acts. Virtual reality again. It doesn't help.

I learned early in my own life that I could withstand difficulty. That was a gift from a disadvantaged childhood. But even with an advantaged childhood, or adulthood, you can begin to increase your self-confidence by simply making decisions and engaging in problem solving, rather than waiting to find the best, the most, the safest.

In addition to stepping aside when your child is faced with an ordinary life problem, as a parent you can plan family meetings once a week where you and your children discuss household and personal problems.[5] Even preschool children should be included. After a check-in, when everyone offers news about the past week, individuals should be invited to bring up problems. Parents should follow the rules Jeannie Norris outlines and simply ask questions about a child's thoughts rather than problem-solve. But when there are difficult family problems—such as not having enough funds for some necessity, having an ill pet, being worried about a sick grandparent or neighbor—everyone should be invited to brainstorm on making a decision about what to do as a group. In this process a lot is learned about idealism, mistakes, and problem solving. Furthermore, family meetings can be a unique opportunity for children to hear about the ordinary difficulties of life.

Ordinary Discontent and Necessary Suffering

In chapter one I introduced the idea that human life always includes discontent and adversity. The original term used by the Buddha to convey this idea is rendered in Sanskrit as *dukkha*. I mention it here because there is no equivalent word for its meaning in English, even though dukkha is usually translated as "suffering." In fact dukkha refers to a quality of experience that we all recognize. It's that feeling of being thrown off-center, like a wheel riding off its axle or a bone riding slightly out of the socket. People can easily feel thrown off the axis of their being, and then nothing seems quite right. Agitation and irritation pervade unless we know how to calm ourselves. This kind of experience occurs all the time. Today, for example, I went into town but forgot my wallet and couldn't run an errand; our water heater broke and started putting out rusty water; there was nothing to eat in the refrigerator when I looked; and I was disappointed in a communication from a friend. On an even more minute level, I've had various aches and pains and a little dyspepsia. And this was a good day! These are the ordinary disgruntlements that come with being alive.

More notable are the big losses and disappointments, such as when we are betrayed by a loved one, when we're diagnosed with a serious illness, when we lose the possibility of pursuing a goal for which we've been preparing a long time, when someone we love dies or experiences a tragedy, and so on. You've suffered some of these, as have I. The familiar and fundamental off-centeredness of dukkha can range from ordinary physical pains and psychological difficulties to the negativity we feel when things and people do not measure up to our ideals, the terrible grief or agony that accompanies abuse or tragedy, or the existential anxiety we confront when we think about losing everything in death. All of these forms of dukkha are built into human existence.[6] Everyone suffers from them; no one is exempt.

When children are repeatedly protected from life's expectable adversities by parents who want them to be happy all the time, the children will assume that ordinary difficulties are extraordinary when they do occur. If a young child has never faced failure, even in playing games or competing with friends, then being called out in her first Little League game will be a self-esteem trap and feel like ignominy. If we're led to believe that we should be mostly happy and get what we want from life, we'll blame ourselves or someone else when this doesn't happen, although it's probably just the way the chips are falling. No amount of material possessions or success can protect us from the limitations of reality—that we'll get ill and die, that things change, and that we have very little control over how people see us and what happens to us. Many young adults find themselves in the self-esteem trap when they leave the protection of their parents because they have no confidence in their own problem-solving skills or their ability to learn from or overcome adversity.

Erik Thompson has been studying young people who are trying to leave home at the end of adolescence or are going through some other kind of social separation. The two of us agree that autonomy—the ability to guide yourself by your own decisions—is a skill that must grow from earliest childhood until emancipation (leaving parents to live on your own) in order for a young person to be confident of leaving home. The young child needs the most protection, of course, but the developing child should make more and more decisions—dealing with self-care, grooming, personal money management, homework, grades, and college applications—in preparing to leave.

Thompson's research revolves around the topic of the self-injurious behaviors that we now see in epidemic proportions among children. He defines self-injurious as cutting, self-mutilation, and parasuicidal behavior, which means thinking and talking a lot about suicide, and taking nonlethal overdoses. "It's pretty widespread. I see it all over," Erik says.[7]

Thompson believes these behaviors are an unconscious communication of protest against separation, an unhealthy sign that these young people feel emotionally unprepared to stand on their own two legs because, he claims, their parents have been running interference too much. "It's like a tantrum that a toddler has. Jane Goodall describes something like this among wild chimpanzees. When a mother is not strong enough to resist the self-attacks that a young chimp may make in protest over being weaned, and takes him back to her breast, this weakens him, and he may never be able to thrive among his peers.[8] In a lot of my early interviews with families, there was a parent, often the father, who was overinvested in a child's homework." He remembered a father who admitted with shame that he had been doing homework for his high school–aged daughter because he didn't want her to fail at anything. She was actually a very good student. The father had started doing his daughter's homework when she was in junior high school. When she was nineteen and moved away to college, she started cutting herself and taking overdoses of medicines, eventually threatening to commit suicide. As Thompson says, it was an unconscious message of "I can't stand on my own two feet. Please rescue me." And in fact her father took an apartment near her college so that he could be available to her, but that only made things worse.

In his clinical work with parents, Thompson warns them of the dire consequences that can come from interfering with children's ability to solve problems for themselves. "That projection of parental anxiety onto children, seeing them as too weak to deal with the consequences of their own actions, is completely hidden from our view. It's under the radar, but it's a force that can really undermine a developing child."

Similarly, when I do therapy with parents of middle school and high school students, I emphasize that children at this age are learning to be autonomous as much as they are learning any subject in school. As I mentioned earlier, autonomy means the ability to govern yourself—to make decisions and be self-determining in your actions. The sooner we expect our children to take responsibility for their actions, whatever their age, the better. At each age there are specific developmental challenges and new responsibilities that are linked to new privileges and freedoms for a growing child. New freedoms—for example, choosing what you will wear or who your friends are—mean new responsibilities in facing the consequences of your choices. If a child is late for school because she dawdled in choosing her clothes and getting dressed, then she should experience the consequence of her tardiness, whatever it is. If a parent steps in (either by rushing the child to school in a speeding car or writing a note to her teacher), then the child has missed the opportunity to take a step toward autonomy in dealing with her own decision making.

What Adversity Teaches

Overcoming adversity and learning from difficulty teach us about suffering, both our own and others'. They also pare down the special self, showing us that often we are not in control of our circumstances, but only (and imperfectly) of our own behavior. Reducing self-blame and keeping faith in ourselves when everything seems to be going against our wishes or desires will allow us to climb out of the self-esteem trap, developing greater empathy and compassion for ourselves and others. Learning the difference between self-blame and responsibility awakens our humility and brings into focus our sense of being ordinary.[9] We begin to understand through our own experience how people always and everywhere struggle with the demands that face them and are frequently thrown off-center in the process.

When this insight sinks in, our hearts open. We see deeply into the fact that no one is protected from change, fear, negative emotions, loss, mistakes, illness, and death. We find it easier to feel confident in our own actions and to be in touch with reality. We also find it easier to relate to others, because we are less afraid of conflict and less inclined to feel negative about our mistakes and foibles. The word "compassion" means literally to suffer with; knowing how to help others comes from suffering yourself. Until you really know what suffering is, you do not know how to help.

In addition to facing and overcoming adversity, we (and our children) also learn from witnessing suffering in others' lives. Well-meaning contemporary parents too often shield their children from others' poverty, serious illness, and death. When parents do so, they are depriving the developing child of understanding adversity and coming into contact with her natural spiritual yearnings. The suffering of others arouses our questions about the meaning of life and death, and eventually ignites our desire to help.

Some parents go against the grain of our culture and decide to expose their children to human misery, sometimes for spiritual reasons and sometimes due to life circumstances. Dr. David Hilfiker, a physician, and his wife, Marja Hilfiker, an educator, made a midlife choice to live among the homeless poor and to serve their needs. In 1983 the Hilfikers moved from a secure middle-class rural life in Minnesota to the Adams-Morgan area of Washington, DC, with their three children: Laurel, twelve, Karin, almost nine, and Kai, four. They joined the small community of the Church of the Saviour, a Christian ministry that serves the poor, worships in small groups (of ten to thirty people), asks that its members donate a minimum of 10 percent of their annual income to the church, and includes a daily practice of contemplation and meditation. Hilfiker has written movingly about his experiences of practicing "poverty medicine" and his spiritual development through living among, and working with, the poor and homeless.[10]

I first heard David Hilfiker on National Public Radio, when he was being interviewed on a show called *Speaking of Faith*.[11] After the catastrophe of the New Orleans flood, the show focused on the urban poor and the spiritual issues they open up for the rest of us. Hilfiker spoke so frankly and insightfully about his work at Christ House, a transitional medical setting in which he served as a doctor for the homeless, and Joseph House, a home for homeless men with AIDS where he was the medical director, that I was transfixed. Also fascinating was his and his wife's experience of raising their three children in these two settings. In Christ House the family had separate quarters where the children could be sequestered away from residents, but at Joseph House their children shared the main living areas with the residents.

I contacted Dr. Hilfiker and interviewed him and his wife in their current apartment in Washington and also interviewed, via e-mail, their middle child, Karin, who has written about spending her teenage years living among the poor and ill. At fourteen, when they moved into the Joseph House, Karin had questions: Would her best friend still come over to visit? Would her boyfriend feel comfortable hanging out? Would any of the men ever become her friends? But soon enough Karin was making friends with her new companions. "It didn't take too long for us to start developing a sense of family. A week or two after our move, all the guys came along with my family to watch me give a ballet recital." She lived in a house where, as she wrote at the age of seventeen, "death visits often," a place where it was not possible "to be happy every moment, but it is possible to *feel* every moment, and that," she wrote, "is what it means to be fully alive." Karin gained an invaluable empathy, compassion, and insight from her life at Joseph House. When she was leaving for her freshman year at Macalester College, in Minnesota, she wrote:

> *How can I be joyful when I live in the midst of so much suffering and death? Because I've learned that suffering is a lot better than indifference. You grieve if you've felt joy. If you're mourning someone's death, it's because you loved someone. If you're mourning*

*the loss of health, it means you've had health. When-
ever you grieve, it's because for a time you have had
something precious, and that is something worth celebrating.*[12]

Karin is now in her early thirties, and when I interviewed her,
I asked her to reflect on what it was like to grow up in the environment of her parents' religious commitment. She responded
that "one of the greatest gifts of living at Christ House and Joseph House was that I was exposed to people, both the staff and
the residents, who were of different races, cultures, and economic
class from my own. I was forced to confront people who were
three times my age and had difficulty reading, who sold drugs,
who robbed people for a living, or who had never left their immediate neighborhood. I was often the only white person. I had
to adapt my speech, mannerisms, and expectations to fit in. For
people of color, this outsider experience is common. Privileged
white folks are used to having other people adapt to them. Having an early view into how people of color and low-income folks
actually approach life and the system was totally eye-opening for
me. It made me aware of how strong the racial divide is in our
culture. I have struggled a lot with this as an adult, but this
awareness has also made it possible for me to form friendships
with, and share community with, people from various racial,
cultural, and economic backgrounds, something I cherish."

Even though Karin admits she's had her share of struggle and
uncertainty in her young adulthood, she says, "I do feel incredibly happy. I have recently finished a degree in physical therapy
and am in my first year of full-time work. I am in a relationship
with a beautiful Indian man who, like me, identifies with communities of color. We've bought a home together in a primarily
Caribbean and American black neighborhood in Brooklyn."

Karin feels grounded in her ability to support her own happiness and confident in her decision making. She sees her struggles as "temporary roadblocks." What stands out in her account of her young life is her certainty about her values, her direction, and her choices. This is a contrast with Adrienne, Erin, and Jason. The sacrifices that were required by her parents' decision to serve the poor provided opportunities for Karin to find herself in an authentic way.

Although Karin's example may seem extreme, it connects adversity, resilience, and wisdom. Human suffering—both the ordinary and the tragic—will awaken spiritual and existential questions and help us recognize the limitations we all face. As parents we must learn to resist the urge to protect and shelter our children from suffering and failures, which provide important opportunities that help them grow into self-confident and wise adults.

In our everyday lives, there are countless opportunities to spend a moment with someone begging on the street, to visit an ill friend or relative, or to tend to a sick or dying pet. Children, even as young as three or four, should come along as witnesses or helpers in these activities. And, of course, these occasions open questions and conversations about the adversity, mistakes, and miseries that everyone suffers eventually.

Help your children to see and notice poverty and differences in privilege that seem inhumane and unfair. Do this in a way that does not increase guilt or shame for what you have as a family, but rather helps them see their responsibility for sharing with others and keeping others in mind. David Hilfiker recalled an event when his son, Kai, then about seven years old, learned something about true poverty. "Kai had made a new friend in our neighborhood when Kai was just learning to ride a bike, someone he invited over to our apartment at Christ House. When his friend left, he stole Kai's bike. First of all, Kai wasn't so distressed, because he figured he'd probably get another bike, but he was impressed with how poor his new friend was. Kai said, 'He really must not have much, because he chose a bike over a friendship.' In that moment, he learned so much about poverty."

Witnessing poverty, bias, or prejudice can be an occasion for children or adults to see beyond their own horizons into another kind of life. Similarly, when a child is expected to perform chores, he should have an opportunity to see beyond his habitual concerns. The reason for chores is to help your child become responsible for others' welfare as well as his own. Find chores that are truly important (for example, caring for a pet or plant) and age-appropriate. Be specific and detailed in showing your child how to do the chore, watch over him for a while, and then let the task be up to your child. Of course, remain in the background as a safety net (don't let the cat die of malnourishment if your son doesn't feed it), but don't take over the responsibility either. Your child should actually feel the negative consequences of not performing a chore or doing it poorly. There is nothing that increases resilience in children more than feeling they are able to perform important tasks and can be depended upon.

Even young children can learn that when adversity throws us off-center, it begins to awaken our own compassion, helping us to learn how to respond skillfully to our own and others' difficulties. Not only does this process lay down a solid foundation for good character and a conscience, it diminishes the sense of entitlement that can come from the unearned privileges of an advantaged childhood. This is what adversity teaches.

CHAPTER FOUR

The Necessity of Conscience and Virtue

Not too long ago my friend's fourteen-year-old daughter shoplifted a cotton T-shirt from a local Gap store. When she bragged about it in an e-mail on the family computer, she got caught by her parents. They asked me what I thought the consequences should be, and I stated what I thought was obvious: she should take the shirt back to the store and ask what she could do to rectify her theft. They were appalled at my suggestion. It would be too humiliating. After all she didn't hurt anyone. Stores like the Gap have insurance policies to cover petty theft. And she'd never do it again. I held my tongue.

Helping a child grow a good conscience is a serious matter that requires a lot of thought and involvement from parents. By the time our children reach their teens—a time of intense and natural self-focus—they will have already formed an identity that says they are either special and superior or an ordinary human being who has to play by the rules. Inflated self-importance and a sense of entitlement make it especially difficult for a teen or young adult to figure out how shoplifting or lying or plagiarizing rips the social fabric on which we all depend, no matter whether you get caught.

Growing a good conscience is a process that begins before the age of six and takes years to fully develop. It starts with rules, and firm guidelines that provide a sensitivity and understanding of the fact that we are interdependent, even in our most private desires and weaknesses. A good conscience is like a compass that will guide us in difficult circumstances when our vision isn't clear.

Growing a Conscience

Conscience is the faculty for recognizing the difference between right and wrong, as well as the desire or motivation to do what is right. The word "conscience" has an old-fashioned ring to it, as if it might not be applicable to our postmodern, busy lives. And yet according to a 2005 survey (the Lichtman/Zogby Poll) of young adults entering the workforce, the overwhelming majority believe that doing the right thing is more important than getting ahead in their careers.[1]

You might think that's good news. Yet despite saying they *want* to do the right thing, when faced with ethical dilemmas, a substantial number of the young adults surveyed say they wouldn't *do* the right thing. For example, 43 percent say they would choose loyalty to friends over being honest. The prisoner abuse scandal at Abu Ghraib is a well-known example in which young Americans compromised their values for loyalty to a friend or coworker. The test of a well-functioning conscience means having the character and courage to do the right thing *even if it costs more than you want to pay*. In fact conscience isn't entirely real until it's tested. Until then it's a set of ideals, or worse, something that is given lip service for the sake of appearance.

Another recent comprehensive survey of almost twenty-five thousand high school students (by the Josephson Institute of Ethics in 2004) showed that nearly two-thirds cheated on tests and 40 percent admitted they "sometimes lie to save money," while more than one in four stole from a store within the past twelve months. And yet just like the young adults, the vast majority of these high school students said that honesty, ethics, and good character are very important to them. In fact 90 percent believed that "being a good person is more important than being rich," and they rejected any cynicism about playing by the rules.[2] This gap between the ideals of good character and the reality of acting ethically piqued my curiosity, and so I decided to conduct an informal survey of young people myself.

At three colleges (one in Massachusetts and two in Vermont), I asked students to respond to a simple questionnaire in which they rated their opinions about lying, cheating, stealing, and being famous or ordinary. My results mirrored the national surveys: the vast majority of respondents felt they should play by the rules, but a considerable percentage struggled with actually doing so. For example, more than a third said they would shoplift in big stores (like Wal-Mart or Gap) if they knew they wouldn't get caught. A whopping 63 percent said that many of their friends lie to their parents and teachers, whereas slightly less than one in four admitted to lying themselves. It was no surprise that more than two out of three said it was better to feel special than ordinary. Thirty percent felt it was hard to be honest because so many people lie. And again, it was no surprise that almost half said they were afraid they wouldn't measure up to the standards they had for the future. Young women were more tempted to shoplift and felt more pressure to be special than young men did.

How can young adults and high school students be so apparently enthusiastic about the importance of good character and ethics and still be so tempted to cheat, lie, and steal? The special self plays a role. On one hand, some young people feel a pressure to succeed in extraordinary ways and hold impossible standards for their success. They may then justify lying, cheating, and stealing because they believe that in "the real world" people do this all the time and that people who are successful have to cheat to get ahead.[3]

On the other hand, they inflate their own self-image in relation to their character. In the survey of almost twenty-five thousand high school students, the researchers concluded that respondents' self-appraisal is flawed: "Despite admissions of high levels of lying, cheating, and theft, high school students maintain a high self-image of their character and ethics both in relative and absolute terms."[4]

When children of well-meaning I'm Okay–You're Okay parents are praised beyond their actual accomplishments and protected from encountering necessary pinches of their young egos, they may develop a burdensome habit of being "entitled."

Entitlement: The Enemy of a Good Conscience

At any age, when people act as if they have rights and privileges they have not earned, others will call them entitled and perceive them as selfish, callous, or offensive. American children are widely seen as entitled and disrespectful of adults. In 2002 only 9 percent of American adults polled said that the children they saw in public were "respectful towards adults," according to a survey done by Public Agenda, a nonpartisan and nonprofit public opinion research group.[5] This is very negative feedback about our children.

Young children—toddlers and preschoolers—may be innocently entitled. They don't yet know the boundaries of their privileges. They are learning with each new occasion of feedback. If we assume we should give in to their demands "because they're powerless and vulnerable," as I've heard some parents say, then we are teaching them that their impulsive aggressions and demands are acceptable, even perhaps what's expected to get their way. When an I'm Okay–You're Okay parent steps in to protect a child from constructive feedback from a stranger, that parent is becoming the problem, as Jeannie Norris says. Eventually the disrespectful behavior that annoyed others will be turned against the parent, often in the child's teenage years.

Using these occasions of innocent entitlement to teach our children the fundamentals of good conscience and care for others is essential. Teach your child a basic moral code and politeness and expect them to be used to make relationships flow more smoothly whenever people are gathered. If you don't know good manners yourself, buy a book and keep it handy. Eventually you can share your book with your child and discuss the reasons for and role of manners in keeping the world moving smoothly.

Emphasize even to your young children that their needs and desires are not always to be the center of attention. The needs of the elderly and the ill trump those of a toddler in most circumstances, and even very young children can learn to respect people who are frail or vulnerable. Most of our adult lives are spent in hierarchies or social groups in which we have to figure out how to relate intelligently to the needs of others as well as ourselves.

This kind of early education takes place in many other cultures. For example, I have traveled in Japan several times over the past ten years and am always shocked to find that children, even very young children, are considerate of my comfort in public places. On a recent trip, a friend of mine (a woman in her sixties) broke her arm. As she and I made our way through the crowds getting on public transportation and moving through the airport—she with her arm in a makeshift sling she'd received at the hospital in Kyoto—we were treated deferentially even by toddlers, who immediately saw her injury and age as a reason to move out of her way or to become silent. It was a big contrast when we stepped off our plane in the Chicago airport, where American high school students pushed my friend out of the way to hurry past her while they were busily chatting among themselves.

Entitlement, unearned privileges, and parental overinvolvement now undermine the motivations that sharpened the conscience of young Americans in the past. Wanting to hear more about today's college students, I had a long conversation with Dr. David Landers, associate professor of psychology at Saint Michael's College, in Colchester, Vermont. Saint Michael's is a Catholic liberal arts college, and I started by asking whether a religious environment makes a difference in problems related to the special self. Landers responded, "Oh no, I don't think so. Catholic students are the same as all the others."

For twenty-three years Landers was the director of the Student Resource Center, the counseling center on campus, but he has now left that post and become visiting associate professor of psychology. A cheerful, large, athletic-looking man in his early sixties, Landers has a warm, energetic manner. When we met he immediately recounted one of his favorite scenes from an episode of *The Cosby Show*. "Bill Cosby's son, on the show, says to his parents, 'We're rich!' and Cosby replies, 'No, you're not rich. Your mother and I are rich. You have nothing.'"

Landers wishes that today's parents could be that brutally honest with their children. "This sense of entitlement—not just with the students, but with the parents too—is rampant. Parents are demanding that we find their kids better accommodations than a dorm room. A friend who has a kid starting college at Saint Michael's told me that she overheard this new freshman girl saying in the dorm bathroom, 'Sharing a bathroom? This is *so* not going to work.' My friend burst out laughing. I told her that I've surveyed my incoming freshmen about how many of them have ever shared a bedroom. Most have not. That's a shift that I've seen over the past ten or twelve years." When privileged children go away to college, they may feel a shock at having to share space and resources with others for the first time in their lives.[6] If parents don't interfere, kids may learn something about kindness and interdependence, but too often helicopter parents run interference.

Young people like Erin, Adrienne, and Jason, as well as the thousands of young people surveyed in the polls I just described, don't know how to guide themselves by the values they have been taught because their expectations aren't realistic. Was Erin's academic mentor, for instance, really inadequate, or was she simply busy with her own research and justifiably unavailable? Erin was unsure. When Erin was working on the sailboat crew for the summer, she neither knew how to protect herself emotionally nor how to assess what was unfair (and should be the subject of complaint). When she looked back at her behaviors in childhood, she said, "I was pretty much a golden child except for back-talking and being a little bit bratty." She didn't really think these counted as bad behavior. Erin felt that she had *earned* the identity of being golden by "just being successful, getting positive feedback, and lots of recognition from grades and teachers."

In fact that "golden" identity came from her elders and others who mirrored back to her the sense that she was almost always good and right, even when she was making mistakes or doing annoying things. I had perfect grades and behaved very politely when I was growing up, but I never had the impression that I was "golden." I was a *child,* for heaven's sake, and knew I couldn't be perfect because everything had such a steep learning curve. I couldn't make a perfect garden, iron a perfect shirt, or wash the floor perfectly without a lot of training and practice. It was clear to me, from an early age, that everything I wanted to do or develop had a *process of mastery* associated with it. But today's children have different and grander expectations. Sometimes these expectations become tragically dangerous.

A Black Hole of Grandiosity

One Saturday in January of 2001, two high school students knocked on the door of the home of Dartmouth University professors Half and Susanne Zantop in Etna, New Hampshire. When Half Zantop came to the door to greet the boys, they said they were doing an environmental survey and asked if the Zantops would help them. Inviting them inside, Half volunteered to help out in any way he could, taking them into his home office. There the boys killed Half and Susanne in a frenzied, bloody murder, plunging hunting knives deeply and repeatedly into their victims. They then took a small sum of money that they found in Half's wallet and left the home, inadvertently leaving behind decisive physical evidence that would lead to their arrest and eventual conviction.

I first heard the news of the "Dartmouth murders" the morning after they occurred, when the headline of our local newspaper caught my eye at the general store where my husband and I routinely stop for cranberry muffins and our morning coffee. Murders are so rare in our area that people have to think back over a decade or two to recall the last one. This one hit close to home, both literally and figuratively. The Zantops lived about forty-five minutes from my home. Although I did not know them personally, I strongly identified with what I read about the murdered couple: two well-educated, loving, dedicated human beings who had devoted their lives to helping young people, as well as to raising their own two daughters. I found myself searching compulsively on the news, and via the general-store gossip grapevine, for any word about who had committed this brutal crime. My neighbors and my therapy clients became frightened and speculated wildly about what kind of out-of-town gang members could be on the loose. When the news broke that two "good boys" from Chelsea, Vermont, were suspects, we were all incredulous. No one could figure out the motive or the circumstances of their involvement.

Gradually the details were released. When the boys, Robert Tulloch and James Parker, left the scene of these horrendous murders, they mistakenly left behind their knife sheaves and a bloody footprint. As the police grew suspicious, the boys planned a getaway and were on their way to California when they were caught. James eventually turned state's witness against Robert, and Robert pleaded guilty without a trial. At the hearing the two young adult Zantop daughters stood before each of the boys and described the dedication and generosity and accomplishments of their cherished parents. James hung his head and wept, but Robert was steely, apparently without emotion. Only James sobbed, "I'm sorry." Because James Parker made a deal with the state, and because he was not the "leader" in the crime, his sentence was softened. He is likely to be released from prison in 2016. Robert Tulloch is in prison for life.

When I finally understood what had actually happened, my sympathies were painfully stirred—naturally for the victims and their loved ones, but also for the parents of the two boys. I found myself flooded with mental images of what it must be like to be a caring and dedicated parent (as these parents were) to a child who commits such a brutal, senseless crime. I came to know that much about the childhoods of the Chelsea boys was not very different from that of my children or the children of my friends. Robert, tall and slim, was a talented senior at the Chelsea School, where he was known to be gifted in mathematics and significantly ahead of the school curriculum in his independent study of philosophers such as Friedrich Nietzsche and Henry David Thoreau. James, with a wide, easy smile, was the cute class clown and a talented drama student. They were doing well in school and not into drinking or drugs. The outer signs seemed to say that these boys were growing up into the young people that their parents and teachers hoped they would become. How, then, could such well-cared-for, promising, and well-liked teenagers commit a frenzied murder?

As part of my research for this book, I read an account of the murders written by two journalists from the *Boston Globe*.[7] From that book and other research, I came to believe that both boys were driven by naive, grandiose expectations and a fear of humiliation. James Parker seemed more naive and submissive, but he went along with Robert's schemes to prove that they were superior to others by stealing or even killing. In the absence of conscience, these two otherwise promising boys were brewing a toxic cocktail of intelligence, cynicism, too little supervision by adults at school, and relentless self-inflation.

So distorted was their self-image that the boys naively thought of Hitler as a kind of role model. He "was a pretty smart guy and was really good at manipulating people," commented James in an interview, adding, "We had a certain amount of respect for him for that. But there was nothing against the Jews."[8] The day they killed the Zantops, Robert and James had headed over to the Hanover, New Hampshire, area (where the town of Etna is) because they wanted revenge for the shameful defeat of the Chelsea School debate team by the Hanover team, in a contest in which Robert had been soundly chastised for being rude.

Robert and James believed that the world operated mostly on dog-eat-dog power schemes, not kindness, compassion, or love. Reflecting back, James said, "We were smarter than everybody else. . . . People didn't see things the way that we did. We thought, you know, what everybody was doing was silly. Like going to school and like wasting half your life with education that you're not going to even use."[9] Robert admired Thomas Jefferson and once remarked to a teacher that Jefferson was a genius but that Jefferson's intelligence paled in comparison with his own "divine intellect." The teacher thought that Robert's hubris was amusing.

The extreme pressure to be famous and superior to others, in the absence of conscience, undermined the humane values and principles that clearly had been taught to the boys by their parents and elders. Robert, especially, was constantly driven by a pressure to prove his intellectual superiority and independence, while James felt the need to attach himself to someone who was really smart and might become famous. Although James Parker did not lay down the plans for their horrible crime, he went along with them because he believed that his friend was a kind of superman, an individual who stood above all others. No one in Chelsea had fundamentally challenged this view of Robert, at least not to Robert's or James's face.

In fact, Andy Pomerantz—once the town doctor of Chelsea and now the chief psychiatrist at the veterans' hospital in White River Junction, Vermont—believes that the town, the teachers, and the community of elders failed these two young men. No adult responded to their arrogance with proper discipline and restraint. The school environment—avoiding "adultism," as described by Dr. Pomerantz in chapter two—did not demand accountability. "Discipline did not exist in the Chelsea School at that time. There was no adult guidance. Once you finished your courses, you could do whatever you wanted," he told me. Robert and James had finished their required courses and so were free to ride around the countryside, scheming about their intellectual superiority.

Looking back at their senseless crime, we may want to imagine that these two teenagers were emotionally ill or otherwise alien. When I asked Dr. Pomerantz what he thought about the *Boston Globe* reporters' claim that Robert was a "psychopath," he said, "That's ridiculous. First of all, he was seventeen years old. A lot of seventeen-year-olds might sound like psychopaths, but they're not. Robert was smart and he had mastered a lot, but he couldn't guide his own life."

A psychopath is by definition a person with an emotional disorder that is motivated by extreme antisocial aggression. Lack of remorse and the absence of conscience are often considered diagnostic.[10] I don't believe that Robert or James was a psychopath in the clinical (as opposed to the popular) sense of the term. They didn't show any signs of such a severe disorder *before* they committed their horrible crime. They could be arrogant and rude, crass and self-promoting, but that was it. The crimes they were scheming were private conversations, sometimes brutal in their imaginings, but also swaggering and naive. The conversations took place in the midst of a social and family life that included the boys' sympathies and care for each other, other people, and pets. Although their example is clearly extreme, it is also instructive: Robert and James's actions were driven by self-inflation and the fear of humiliation, not by psychopathy.

As for the parents of Robert and James, I have not seen any evidence that they grossly failed to be responsible in terms of knowing their kids and their whereabouts. I can put myself in their shoes and imagine that I would have supported the idea that the boys were especially talented, even though too self-important—identifications that the boys held in the community at large. I probably wouldn't have questioned the school's decision to release the boys from their classes after having completed the credits they needed. I assume that the Tullochs and Parkers were I'm Okay–You're Okay parents, like most educated parents are now. I know they cared deeply about their sons and tried hard to raise them well. Short of searching the boys' private computer files, the parents could not have known what was brewing. You may believe that these parents are culpable, having made some fundamental mistakes. I do not. I believe they, like the conscientious parents I see in therapy, were doing all they knew how to do to be good parents. Tragically for everyone involved, they were raising their children in a social climate that looked upon individual achievement and wit as primary markers of success. This climate also encouraged students to feel entitled to privileges and powers because they were special. Of course, that entitlement almost never results in the horrible acts that the Chelsea boys committed. And yet it can often lead to the self-esteem trap of obsessive self-focus, restless dissatisfaction, and the pressure to be exceptional that marked Robert Tulloch and James Parker. This outcome is a stark contrast with the virtue and mastery that dedicated parents and teachers desire as the aim of healthy development.

Virtue and Mastery

Virtue, another old-fashioned word, is the building block of a good moral character; the dictionary defines it as "moral excellence and righteousness."[11] Every list of virtues—whether it comes from a Judeo-Christian, Buddhist, Islamic, or Hindu background—includes honesty, persistence, kindness, patience, courage, gratitude, generosity, and wisdom.[12] Cultivating these virtues in our children and ourselves requires gentle, matter-of-fact attention and dedication. If we overlook the development of virtue and overemphasize self-importance, then we are likely to cultivate the self-esteem trap, without wanting to. People are *always* cultivating something in their minds—anxiety, anger, ruthlessness, self-protection, confusion. If you knowingly attempt to cultivate a virtue, you not only replace your anxiety or confusion with something positive, you also inevitably feel better because your mind is occupied with something other than its own fretting.

My mother frequently said, "Virtue is its own reward," when I complained of someone not returning a kindness I had offered. At these moments she would give what sounded to me like a righteous minilecture about virtue and its consequences. She would say, "When you do something kind, that kindness always comes back to you." Now that I am a middle-aged Buddhist, I hear those previously irritating minilectures as my early teachings about karma, which means simply "the consequences of intentional actions." The Buddha taught that we always reap the consequences of our own actions, most especially the things we do with a specific motive or intention.[13] The Christian tradition teaches the same idea about our motivations. If it is your intention to help someone, for example, and the other person doesn't seem grateful, then you are still rewarded by your own intention. Something good comes from a good intention. If, on the other hand, you pretend to help someone because you want praise or rewards, then you will reap the consequence of your duplicity, even if the other person seems not to notice it. I now look upon my mother's words as wisdom, even though I received them ambivalently, especially in my teenage years.

My mother also frequently reminded me that "patience is the greatest virtue" when I wanted to leap over hard work and practice and quickly be the best at something. In this way she insisted on the value of persistence, as I would now call it. I have found as an adult that my habit of persistence has paid off mightily. My choice to become a psychotherapist and a writer has kept me engaged in two lifelong activities that demand an openhearted willingness to learn from my mistakes. Repeatedly coming back and recommitting myself to a relationship or an endeavor after I have been criticized or critiqued has been one of the best sources of wisdom I have found.

In their book *Character Strengths and Virtues* (2004), the psychologists Christopher Peterson and Martin Seligman remind us of the importance of diligence, patience, and persistence in the development of true creativity, a goal that most dedicated parents hold for their children.

> *For creativity to advance beyond its everyday forms . . .*
> *the individual must acquire considerable expertise*
> *with the chosen domain of creative activity. This need*
> *for expertise acquisition is often expressed as the 10-*
> *year rule. . . . According to this rule, no person can*
> *make creative contributions to a particular domain*
> *without first devoting a full decade to the mastery of*
> *the necessary knowledge and skills.*[14]

Persistence, patience, and a respect for my elders helped me discover that mastery takes time. I learned to let go of my disappointments about myself and keep my eye on the ball of what I was learning.

Young adults today who do not realize that virtues undergird mastery and are required for creativity will prematurely give up on many opportunities because they believe they themselves have a better version of how things should go. If you haven't had to conform to others' needs, learn how to do chores that demand precision, or even meet the consequences of your own mistakes and problems while you are under your parents' roof, you might come to believe that you need to oppose or correct elders who don't share your views about how to accomplish something.

A cross-cultural study of American and Japanese high school students looked at the differences in the stories told about a picture on a test that is routinely used by psychologists to understand children's emotional problems and motivations.[15] The picture is a drawing of a young boy contemplating a violin lying on a table in front of him. The respondent is asked to tell the story of what is going on in the picture, to tap into her or his imagination about the scene. A study of seventeen- and eighteen-year-old Japanese youths at public schools in Japan and American high school students from the top ten public schools in California showed important contrasts. When eighty-five stories from each country were compared, themes of achievement and creativity characterized the Japanese stories, while themes of parental pressure and opposition were dominant among the U.S. teens.

Here's a typical American response, from a young man:

> *"I hate school. It's so boring," thought the boy. Another music lesson. "Why does Mommy make me take violin lessons? I can't play as well as the teacher wants me to.". . . He couldn't stand the long, cold halls of the school. The unfriendly teachers were always berating him for this or that.*[16]

The Japanese themes were the opposite of the American stories. They tended not to emphasize the negativity of hard work, but the reason or motivation behind it, and the ability to succeed. Typically the stories combined the child's own desire to achieve with a feeling of positive regard for the family. For example, one young man said,

> *He's looking at the violin which is a memento from his grandfather. He's thinking about this grandfather, and talking to his spirit. He will practice and will succeed greatly as a violinist.*

And a Japanese girl replied to the picture on the card,

> *The boy is said to be a musical genius. He has been practicing late and has a headache. He is massaging his temple. His headache has not disappeared. Recalling his mother's advice not to work too hard, he will take some medication and go to bed.*[17]

The American high school students told stories that showed negative feelings toward parents and teachers who were demanding or even manipulating the boy's achievements, but the Japanese students told stories about the boy's wanting to master the violin for himself. His teachers and parents were respected for helping him, but his own persistence and diligence were the driving forces.

We don't often associate virtue with creativity and self-determination, but it turns out that virtue is necessary for these other resources to work. And it's not just because we can guide ourselves more readily in knowing what to choose, but because we can master the developmental processes that are important for our success. Peterson and Seligman tell a story of diligence and patience about a famous teenager: sixteen-year-old John D. Rockefeller, who needed a job in the summer of 1855. Having finished a three-month bookkeeping course, the ambitious young Rockefeller—a poor working-class youth living in Cleveland—put together a list of businesses there that might need his services. There were plenty of places to choose from, and Rockefeller, clad in coat and tie, spent several hot summer weeks walking from business to business. He was rejected by every one of them. Rather than feeling defeated by humiliation, though, he began again, going back to each firm that had rejected him and asking for another interview. Eventually a shipping company hired him. Rockefeller's persistence paid off over his lifetime, as he became one of the richest and most powerful businessmen in the world.[18] Many of today's young adults want these successful results and may claim also to want the virtues and good character that are needed to accomplish them. And yet today's youth feel a pressure to take shortcuts by cheating and lying, not recognizing that the shortcuts actually rob them of the needed virtue and mastery.

How Entitlement Is Linked to Cheating and Lying

Even young adults themselves complain about the entitlement of their generation, often about those just a few years younger than themselves. I talked with thirty-one-year-old Kyle from Seattle, who went out there to work in the software industry, about his views of his generation. "Many kids have had parents who have indulged them to such a degree that their expectations of the world are completely out of alignment with what is really possible," he said, expressing disappointment with his own and the younger generation. "This gets reinforced through the media, television, movies, and even our own educational and psychological systems. There seems to be no tolerance for negative experiences, even pain itself. People my age fear depression like the plague because they've been taught that unless they are excelling and feeling completely confident, there must be a problem."

When I asked Kyle what role moral or ethical values play in this problem, he said, "Kids my age tend to see ethics only in identity or self-oriented terms. For instance we want fairness in treating people of different sexual orientation or race equally. Which is fine, but there is a bigger picture of what's required to be an ethical person. We shouldn't do harm to others, no matter what. That seems to be lost on us. The Golden Rule and the Ten Commandments seem to be lost on many of us. In place of these are interests in various mythical or ritual identities [from movies, role-playing, and video games] that don't carry much ethical meaning." Kyle also thought that people his age probably cheat more in relationships and on tests than previous generations did. He thinks this kind of cheating goes along with shoplifting and lying because "young people now think they're *owed* something even if they haven't earned it. Lying is so common that it's hard for me to tell what is and isn't true when my friends talk about their accomplishments."

Young children innocently and naturally believe that exaggerating their accomplishments or trying to erase their faults is harmless to others. Only over a long period of maturation do children develop the capacity to identify the actual flaw of lying: that it rips the social fabric and undermines our trust in one another. As the famous child developmentalist Jean Piaget discovered, the problem with lying is difficult for children to discern. At the age of three or four years, a child perceives a lie as "a naughty word" and confuses lies with other bad words, for example cursing, for which she may receive punishment or irritation from adults. According to Piaget in his 1965 book, *The Moral Judgment of the Child:*

Naturally inclined as he is to think about himself rather than about others, the child does not see the full significance of deceit. He lies as he romances, so that the obligation not to lie, imposed upon him by adult constraint, appears from the first in its most external form . . . independently of the subject's intentions.[19]

A more advanced definition of a lie tends to emerge sometime between the ages of six and ten years: a lie is something we say that isn't true. This definition seems to include an appreciation of the intentional aspect of lying, saying something we know is not true. But still, although the definition seems to express an adult view, Piaget cautions that most children continue to confuse lies and mistakes. Even though mistakes may be noted by children as different from lies proper, mistakes are still often fused with lies in a child's reasoning. For example, a child of seven might say that an untrue statement is "a lie and a mistake." The confusion between a lie and a mistake begins to disappear around the age of eight, but children continue to be unclear about the social meaning of lying until they are about eleven. At this point they have sufficient chronological maturity to understand that a lie is intentional and destroys another's trust in our words.

Not until the end of adolescence, however, at about the age of nineteen or twenty, can an individual have the full intellectual and emotional capacity to appreciate how and why being truthful and trustworthy contributes to a sense of ease and mastery in life.[20] This ability does not grow naturally or biologically. It must be cultivated. Piaget emphasizes the importance of cooperating with others in developing a mature conscience. When we share and cooperate, we begin to learn how helping others and being honest also benefit the self. GenMe young people may not have learned these lessons by the time they arrive at college. Their self-importance and the self-esteem trap can produce moral functioning that is immature for their age.

The Value of Authenticity

Several college professors expressed the sentiment that Kyle did about GenMe'ers. Students feel entitled to success and tangible results, no matter how they get them. "My students are incredibly strong in consumer skills," says Gigi Marks, a writing professor who primarily teaches creative writing at Ithaca College, in upstate New York.[21] Because she often asks students to write about themselves, she has a unique window into their personal worlds.

"In the last five years, I've seen a change in the way students, especially female students, demand good grades for paying their fees and doing assignments. It would have been too humiliating in the past to show up at a professor's door demanding a higher grade, but that's changed. There's no sense of earning a grade. If you pay and do the work, you expect to get a good grade." Professor Marks feels that the demand for grades is connected to something darker than the desire for success. "Many of my students live in a world that is, in its way, postcynical. They read and write because they are told to do so in order to get a grade. They don't necessarily see the assignments as meaningful in themselves. Fewer students than in the past seem to recognize the importance of process rather than product." When she asks them to write on topics they don't know about or to do an assignment that goes against their usual habits, they are baffled. Why should they do that? They want the grade, not the process of mastery.

Professor Marks believes self-importance and entitlement have obscured the students' appreciation of the worth of authenticity. Like honesty, authenticity is a virtue that is initially hard to understand from the outside. If you're focused on external success, manipulating others, or status, it's very hard to see the value of being authentic: the quality of being transparent and open, honest and genuine. As any good antique dealer knows, when something is authentic, it is genuine, worthy of trust, and grounded in truth or fact.

Professor Marks believes, as Kyle does, that the children of I'm Okay–You're Okay parents might cheat more in relationships and on tests because they don't understand the value of learning from negative feedback and owning up to mistakes and failures. These GenMe'ers have grown up with a primary focus on their own success: get my grades, win my games, visit my friends. Their childish egocentrism may continue into late adolescence and young adulthood because it has been unwittingly enhanced by an overfocus on individual opportunity or success.

Professor Marks told me about a topic that her students had chosen for writing a personal essay: lying to parents. "In a class of twenty students, everybody, of course, had lied to their parents, and most students assumed that would be the case. They didn't think it was unusual to lie, except for one student, a young man born in America to Vietnamese parents. He wrote about a time he had lied to his parents and the mortification he experienced because he had lied. Even though he would not necessarily erase the lie itself, he felt there was something deeply wrong with lying." In his essay, this young man expressed remorse that he had committed this trespass of his values. Professor Marks asked the student to read his essay out loud to the class. "He didn't want to do it at first, but finally he did, and the essay and the reading of it were beautiful. The other students were shocked in a pretty open way. It was nothing they would have ever come up with themselves."

As we have seen, the fundamental problem with lying is that

it rips the moral fabric and prevents authenticity and trust between us. If we cannot believe each other's words, if there is no real transparency, then we cannot rely on our communications. Once we have cut off this lifeline of open communication, we are adrift and cannot connect with the vitality of interdependence. Again, Gigi Marks: "I recently read an essay by one of my better students, a reasonably talented writer, about how he sees himself primarily as a liar. He found this habit of lying deeply problematic because he could not find out who he truly was. But he also said that lying was the way he felt he could move through the world most successfully, using this currency of lies. It was very sad for me because he is talented."

Gigi Marks ties this dishonesty into yet another problem of authenticity: cheating in romantic or sexual relationships.[22] "It seems like there's always tension about cheating, worrying about cheating, or thinking about cheating on your partner or girlfriend or boyfriend—and then not telling them about the trespass. It's so much more than I would have expected. I have a very bright student whose parents are very accomplished. She was writing about cheating on her boyfriend in a way that expressed the cheating as having so little importance to her or to him. There were real trespasses. She has a vocabulary of caring, she knew the words, but she didn't get some very basic tenets of authenticity and honesty."

The Foundation of Conscience

In order for children to grow up with a reasonable chance of becoming authentic, morally mature adults, they need the foundation of conscience. A good conscience, grounded in virtues, will promote a growing appreciation for the central role that trust plays in happiness and ease. Conscience, as we have seen, includes both the knowledge of right and wrong and the desire to do what is right.

The knowledge of right and wrong has to be learned first as a constraint, a limitation on the normal egocentrism of childhood. Traditionally this has been handled through religion. In later chapters we'll turn to the topics of religion, reverence, and compassion to understand their contributions to conscience and virtue in today's world.

Beyond knowing the rules of right and wrong, children have to learn the lessons of living cooperatively and sharing that will help them to embrace the spirit, rather than conform to the letter, of the rules that provide for transparency and openness in human relationships. Look for opportunities to cultivate an awareness of interdependence—of all of the ways we are dependent on others—and gratitude for what others provide us. For instance, in eating with a child, speak often and with interest about all that has gone into bringing food to the table. Start with the insects and the soil and follow all the many transformations that take place (through people and other creatures) until the food reaches the table. This shows your child a palpable example of how connected we are to others—other people and other beings—who may be invisible but are essential to our lives. Developing this account of interdependence over many mealtimes, and visits to farms and food factories, will sensitize your child to the toil and care that go into every meal. Then it becomes natural to feel gratitude to those whose toil is of such benefit, and a deep sadness in wasting food; it wastes the work of so many. There are dozens of resources that we use every day that connect us to others who are invisible but essential. Tell those stories to your child.

Feeling gratitude for what has been provided allows us to be generous and vice versa. Acting on our generosity in giving to others will expand our gratitude for what has helped us. In your personal interactions with your child, help her find ways to express her generosity in thinking of gifts or communications for others who have helped her—beyond the set of friends with whom she normally interacts.

From the horrible story of the Dartmouth murders, we recognize how powerful self-importance can become when its desires are fed by unrealistic longings and unchallenged by moral constraints. As we'll see in the next chapter, there is a moment in adolescence when our developing autonomy and self-reflective capacities join up with an identity that formed in our first ten or eleven years. If a child has been repeatedly told or made to feel better, smarter, or more talented than others, that child is likely to identify with being special and entitled to certain privileges and resources. However, if the foundation for moral development has been cultivated, with kindness and respect for others, then it's more likely that a growing conscience can guide a child as the powerful self-conscious forces of later adolescence sweep in.

CHAPTER FIVE

Autonomy and Emotional Maturity

Recently my friend Shannon, the mother of an eight-year-old daughter, was looking ahead to those scary adolescent years that often torment parents. Shannon is lucky because she has a wide range of friends with children of different ages, including quite a few who are guiding their teenage children into young adulthood. They've "been there, done that" when it comes to the fears of adolescence. One woman in particular, speaking about sending her son off to college, said something that was a wake-up call for Shannon: "I didn't raise him to keep him." At that moment Shannon was hit by the fact that she was actually raising her eight-year-old to leave home.

I immediately thought about some of my therapy clients and my friends whose children have moved back home after graduating from college.[1] Those parents believed they too were raising their children to leave home, but things haven't quite worked out that way. If children, teens, or young adults are trapped in fragile self-importance and are morally or emotionally immature, what can be done to strengthen their maturity muscles? And what prepares children to stand on their own anyway?

You'll recall that I mentioned in chapter one the critical importance of autonomy to our emotional maturity as adults: autonomy is the metaphorical muscle that allows us to stand on our own, knowing our strengths and weaknesses. Beginning in childhood and continuing throughout our lives, our autonomy is our ability to be self-determining and self-governing. Our individual freedom to make choices and to commit ourselves to those choices is one of the delights of living a human life. Other animals are driven more strongly by their instincts, but we humans have the unique capacity to abstract ourselves from our immediate experience and take a larger view in order to make a choice that may or may not reflect our instincts, impulses, and urges. We've seen how adversity, conscience, and virtue make important contributions to our using this freedom wisely. Keep in mind that robust self-confidence, self-esteem, and resilience are founded on learning early and repeatedly that our happiness depends on knowing how to be responsible for ourselves and our commitments.

Shannon is still in the midst of parenting a young child, making lots of decisions for her: "Making sure her clothes match, negotiating how much to eat of dinner before she can have dessert, picking up playthings off the floor, seeing that she brushes her teeth. So much has been under my control, from the friends she has, to the clothes she wears, to when she goes to bed. What I woke up to is that I need to start teaching my daughter now about making decisions for herself." What Shannon woke up to was that even by the age of eight, children need to begin to exercise their autonomy muscles. Shannon's daughter should already be making some decisions—choosing what clothes to wear and having some freedom to pick her friends—and, most important, encountering the consequences of her own decisions.

Autonomy: Past and Present

When we govern ourselves effectively, we are able to take on all that life delivers—both bad and good—and know how to respond through our speech and actions. This does not mean that we are independent of others or their influences, but rather that we know when and how to negotiate our responsibilities and needs. Although we continue to build and refine our autonomy throughout our adult lives, its foundations are laid down in adolescence, a time of naturally intense egocentrism and self-concern. The identity we first formed in our childhood years—the feelings and images we have of ourselves—meets up with a big dose of self-consciousness when our brain begins to change in adolescence.

Around the age of eleven, children's capacity to make decisions for themselves reaches a new level of maturity with changes in brain development.[2] This is an especially key moment for parents to step back from meddling in age-appropriate personal decisions for their children. Children should make their own choices, and deal directly with the consequences, in doing their homework on time, studying for tests, working out a quarrel with a friend. In all of these arenas, parents need to allow children to spend time in reflective misery when things don't go their way. For the I'm Okay–You're Okay parent, this means tolerating the empathic frustration, anguish, or anxiety that your children's negative feelings arouse in you. Taking a mature view, a parent can become more objective and recognize that facing adversity is a part of growing up. Failures and mishaps teach us about ourselves and about the world—how others see us and what we can expect. By late adolescence, a child's autonomy should include taking all of the consequences (without parental interference) of poor school performance, social difficulties, il-

legal drug and alcohol use, minor shoplifting, and plagiarizing—the typical kinds of problems that I'm Okay–You're Okay
parents try to cover up or smooth over. When adults don't run
interference, even if there's a struggle, this eventually produces a
positive effect on a teen's emerging self-confidence and ability to
work with the reality of an imperfect world.

I've mentioned that weekly family meetings (that should ide-
ally include all who live in the home, even if they are not biological relatives) provide an arena in which hierarchy, honesty,
compassion, and interdependence can be witnessed by children
in adults, and can be taught to children by adults. Meetings are
a good place to air problems and failures of individuals, as well
as the conflicts and tasks that everyone shares in making a life
together. Family meetings should provide an atmosphere in
which it's clear to all that talking about personal limitations and
mistakes is helpful, not shameful.

Adults can set an example by bringing up what they struggle
with and asking others in the family for any suggestions they
might have. Although adults should primarily empathize with
children's feelings and not problem-solve, if a child specifically
asks that others in the family give some suggestions or advice for
coping with a problem, then a parent, older sibling, or other
elder can briefly share some wisdom from her or his own experience.

Of course, it's the job of teenagers, especially young teens, to
feel they are the center of everything and that everyone is watching them. That won't ever change, because it's built into our biology.[3] What has changed, though, is the way adults respond to
this kind of self-concern. When I was growing up, my mother
would say some version of "Get over yourself, you look *just
fine*" when I was fishing for a compliment or worried about my
appearance. "Beauty is as beauty does" and "You can't hide a

light under a bushel basket" were a couple of the aphorisms that parents fed back to teenage Boomers when they wondered about their appearance or intelligence. These sayings imply that modesty and good character are more important than being top dog. Many children growing up now, and those who are in young adulthood, wouldn't know how to relate to such sayings, except perhaps to be insulted. Today's GenMe'ers mistakenly believe that status, self-focus, celebrity, and power are the keys to autonomy, and they expect to have their parents' support in reaching for them. Sadly these very concerns set them up for the self-esteem trap with its hair trigger for humiliation.

The other evening, when my husband and I attended a local performance of Thornton Wilder's play *Our Town,* I was shocked by the change in how I felt during the scenes in which the teenage children are parented. The audience is meant to feel it is looking in on an average American household, identifying with the parents and the children. It must have been twenty years since I last saw the play, which was first performed in 1938. At those earlier times when I was in the audience—in high school, college, and when my children were youngsters—I easily accepted the parents' voices as natural and authentic. This time, though, I felt a disconnect, thinking, "No one disciplines children like *that* or expects that level of obedience." Seeing the play gave me a visceral recall of how much more parents demanded of their children not long ago, and how much less indulgent parents were about chores and responsibilities.

Children who have grown up with today's I'm Okay–You're Okay parenting, feeling entitled to all sorts of resources, struggle with needing a lot of compliments and expecting unearned privileges.[4] It's often unclear to them what their responsibilities are to their families and communities. And if they haven't ever failed at anything or been made to feel that they didn't know what they were doing, then it might seem unbearable to receive a rejection—be it from a college, a job, or a lover. Because they haven't had to experience feeling let down, they don't know how to cope with it successfully. They just expect the ideal from others and themselves.

"We Gen X/Y'ers, as I like to call us," remarks thirty-one-year-old Kyle from Seattle, "think of ourselves as progressive and future-thinking, but the pressure to conform to idealized standards is our predominant theme. Unless you feel you are excelling in life, you feel like you're failing." This is one reason some of today's capable young people, who appear to be well prepared for adult life, often step back from a timely entrance into earning a living, committing to a partner, raising a family.

The pressure to be ideal comes in part, as we have seen, from the efforts of parents and other adults to protect children from experiencing their own failures and mistakes. Overpraising and running interference weaken the legs that our children need to stand on when they leave home. Caught in the self-esteem trap, young adults find themselves having two contradictory identities: special and defective. On the one hand, they believe they should be, or are, superior to others, but on the other hand, they can't tolerate the slightest criticism or failure without feeling humiliated or defeated. They fear they don't have what it takes to stand up to life.

Self-Consciousness and Fear of Failure

Thirty-two-year-old Andrew entered psychotherapy when he was twenty-eight.[5] His story follows the general outline of Adrienne's and Erin's. Tall, blond, and athletic, Andrew had the kind of striking good looks that seemed to promise a certain degree of self-confidence that he did not possess. His dress, mostly black and casual, reflected an artistic style that blended surprisingly well with his athletic body; he had been a serious competitive tennis player throughout his high school years. And yet this confident-looking young man spent six years after his graduation from an Ivy League college in a series of negligible jobs and often felt overwhelmed with insecurity in relationships with women. On Prozac for the past six years—and reluctant to even consider the possibility of ever stopping because he thought it kept him going—Andrew was insecure and uncertain about himself. My knowledge of Andrew comes primarily from what his therapist has written about him, supplemented by an essay written by Andrew himself.

For all the years Andrew could remember, his father had preached about the importance of Andrew's having work that really interested him; to do otherwise would be "soul murder." Highest on Andrew's list of priorities was art. He had studied painting, film, furniture design, and construction at various times in his young adulthood. Whatever he tried, though, Andrew was left with the belief that he couldn't produce anything exceptional enough to make it worth staying in the field. Andrew obviously had never heard of Peterson and Seligman's ten-year rule, that no one can make a truly creative contribution to a field without first devoting a full decade to mastering the field. Andrew felt that he failed if he didn't produce something spectacular after just a few months, even weeks, in a new endeavor.

Andrew is like many of the creative writing students taught by Professor Gigi Marks at Ithaca College. "So many of my students feel that if they don't become successful quickly—publishing at least one book by their late twenties—their lives will be empty and meaningless. I think it must be very frightening to feel this way. In response I tell them that in order to be a writer, they have to hang in there and wait for something to happen. Have a full life and keep coming back to your writing. They don't listen to me about this. Instead they think of themselves as serious writers at a very young age, not as writers in training. They seem to believe it's more important to be exceptional than to learn things."

A recent survey showed that a stunning 98 percent of college freshmen agreed with the statement "I am sure that one day I will get to where I want to be in life."[6] This belief has led to delusional ambitions among young people who regularly predict they will be famous, exceptionally creative, well educated, or make a lot of money. The pressure to achieve great things results in high levels of anxiety and depression. Psychologist Jean Twenge, in her book *Generation Me,* reports that "only 1% to 2% of Americans born before 1915 experienced a major depressive episode during their lifetimes, even though they lived through the Great Depression and two world wars. Today, the lifetime rate of major depression is ten times higher—between 15% and 20%. Some studies put the figure closer to 50%."[7] During 2002 alone, 8.5 percent of Americans took an antidepressant drug.[8] Twenge also found that anxiety increased so much in the 1990s that the average college student was more anxious than 85 percent of students in the 1950s and 71 percent of students in the 1970s.[9]

The pressure to achieve quickly was characteristic of Andrew. He came to therapy because he had enrolled in a graduate program in architecture and was tormented by the fear that in doing so he had sacrificed his true calling to be a painter. He hoped that therapy might help him persist in architecture or clarify that he was abandoning his "true self," the painter. In any case Andrew did recognize that his desire to flee architecture school just after he had enrolled was probably a personal problem, not primarily something about the program.

Andrew's other problem was his relationship with a young woman he'd met at his Ivy League college. Cathy, who had her own idealistic visions for the future, decided that she needed to live in Paris. Andrew, who had been living with her for a few years after college, agreed to move with her, although he knew he couldn't get work for himself there. When things didn't go as she had expected, Cathy became a shut-in, staying in bed all day, crying, and insisting that her life would be hopeless unless Andrew pledged himself to her, no matter what. Eventually, after Cathy repeatedly rejected him sexually, Andrew discovered she was having an affair. He wanted her to stop, but she insisted that the affair was meaningless and that she really loved Andrew. He was extremely humiliated and upset by her continuing the affair and refusing sex with him, but Andrew stayed on in Paris for a good while, trying to believe that Cathy's affair had nothing to do with their relationship.

In his shame, Andrew remained bound up with Cathy for several years, even after he moved back to the States and was in therapy. When his therapist expressed his own anger with Cathy for having treated Andrew so badly, Andrew was shocked. He had been oblivious to his anger, hidden by shame as it was. Over quite a long time, he was completely unable to set limits on Cathy's behavior, although he was fully aware that she was manipulating him.

Shame is the sense or belief that something is wrong with the self, something is defective or missing. Distinctly different from guilt (the knowledge that we have acted badly and can repair things by acting well), shame can bring on a downward spiral in which we become immobilized because we believe the self is fundamentally defective—and hence we are unable to do what is demanded or expected. This immobilization produces evidence that something *is* wrong, often leading to a desire to hide, disappear, or die. At this point a person might receive the diagnosis of depression from a psychiatrist and be prescribed antidepressant medication, as Andrew was.

Through his therapy Andrew began to feel more autonomous. He discovered his shame and fear of failure—and his refusal to use his own anger to protect himself and move forward in his life. He began to trust his ability to make good decisions and to stay the course even when those decisions made his life more difficult in the short run. He was able to break up with Cathy and eventually to enter into a healthier relationship. Andrew also discovered that his struggle to find a career included a confusion between work and recreation. Andrew's eyes were opened by the idea that work was about earning a living. Repeatedly in his adult life, he had received financial support from his wealthy father. These handouts increased both his shame and his confusion about his career desires and possibilities.

Andrew had for many years felt unclear about how to guide himself and do what would be expected of an adult. After four years of intensive psychotherapy, he writes:

> *My problems have always been that I am afraid of people criticizing me and realizing my weaknesses, my inferiority. I am afraid of women, of exhibiting my sexual desire to them, of making an idiot out of myself, of taking risks that may make me vulnerable in any way to criticism. To a certain extent, I have taken paths around these fears instead of confronting them. And what I have done about these fears in the past is to feel sorry for myself that I had them and assume no one else had them. Now I realize that I, like everyone else, just have to accept that those fears exist and confront them as best as possible.*[10]

With his therapist's help, Andrew was able to finish architecture school, which included many ego-shattering critiques that were conducted in a group setting. "Architecture school demanded that I produce quickly and efficiently, something that I always had a hard time accomplishing. I was riddled with thoughts of my own inferiority with respect to other students and to the criticism that was liberally dealt out." [11]

Prior to therapy Andrew lacked the inner voice that would allow him to evaluate his own work in relation to what others were saying about it and to see whether or not it was worthwhile. Too often absorbed with negative self-assessment, shame, or unrealistic goals, Andrew wasn't able to guide himself. As we have repeatedly seen, entitlement, overpraise, and overprotection can become obstacles in the process of a teenager's developing ability to take an overview of himself. I often call this overview the "view from the balcony," as one of my clients once dubbed it.

Our View from the Balcony

This broader self-reflective view is what Freud and others have called the superego—in literal translation from the German *Über-ich,* the "over-I." [12] A realistic view from our balcony and a healthy conscience foster the inner voice that allows us to navigate our own course, to know our own strengths and weaknesses, and to know how to respond usefully to others' criticisms of us. This is the voice of conscience, intuition, and wisdom, as well as self-knowledge. Learning to hear it and tune into it takes training and practice. Cut off from this voice, young adults are susceptible to feelings of shame and failure when they should be feeling something else—curiosity, at least, about whatever is happening. As Andrew notes, "My own ability to evaluate my work was lacking. But through my therapy, by the time I was in my last semester I was able to give my own design work enough legitimacy to carry it out effectively." [13]

When Andrew thinks back over his young life, he wonders what would have become of him if he had not gotten into intensive psychotherapy (three sessions per week) that helped him achieve a newfound autonomy. He says,

> *Would I have stayed in graduate school? Would I have retreated to the same relationship that had bled me dry of self-esteem, a healthy sex life, and any drive to make a productive and happy life for myself? Would I be living at home? Would I be sucking down Prozac in hopes that it would treat any and all unhappiness in my life related to love and work and money?*[14]

What Andrew is asking himself involves how we see ourselves in relation to the world and others, the way we sustain the hope that we can succeed and offer something worthwhile, even as we are being frustrated by our circumstances or criticized by others. Developing a reliable capacity to guide ourselves, taking an overview, is a long and complex process for human beings.

The dependency of childhood is much longer and more ambivalent for a human being than for any other animal on earth. Human children are the only creatures to have the long-term demands of many different developmental periods, with highly contrasting aims. Human parents have an even more difficult task before them, in preparing their young for autonomy, than those penguin parents in the recent popular documentary *March of the Penguins,* who hold their eggs delicately between their feet in subzero temperatures.

The Delicacy of Identity

The human brain has many capacities that can unfold *only* in the context of ongoing human relationships.[15] These capacities are first wholly influenced, and can readily be distorted, by the support and guidance that parents provide. The diverse developmental strands of a human childhood should culminate in our autonomy, the ability to know how to govern ourselves in our actions and speech.

We build our autonomy from the ground of our identity—how we see ourselves. From this ground we gauge our responsibilities and connections to others. Our identity is primarily shaped by two things: how our significant others have created us in their imaginations (and conveyed these views implicitly and explicitly) and what we've directly learned from the consequences of our actions in our relationships and endeavors.

Our significant others begin to create our identity before we are born. We are talked about, planned for, and imagined by others before we appear. We are often given our names (which link us to a background of meaning) and shaped by our parents' dreams before we pop out of our mother's body.[16] Between conception and around eighteen months of age, the biology of a young child drives normal developmental processes that unpack the human brain through relationships (at first from inside the mother's body). Unless there is some anomaly in this earliest phase, the force of nature plays a strong hand. And yet even at this stage, the infant largely depends on interactions with others for its sense of itself and its worth in addition to its sustenance.

In the first eighteen months after birth, while the internal life of the infant is unfolding, the social drama of family—including the envy and rivalry of siblings and the circumstances and wishes of parents—is rolling along. The newest member of the group is unable to know it yet, but he or she already has a role assigned. Family life is like a theater in which each member plays a part, including the person coming onstage for the first time. The beliefs that other family members have about us, our place in the sibling order, and the historical moment will dictate aspects of our identity that shape us long before we become active.[17] The historical moment alone has much more influence than we think. The psychologist Jean Twenge found, in her intergenerational research on 1.3 million young Americans, that "*when* you were born has more influence on your personality than the family who raised you. Or, in the words of a prescient Arab proverb, 'Men resemble the times more than they resemble their fathers.' "[18]

By the age of three or so, a young child has a definite experience of being an individual, separate from others—being "in here" while the world and others are "out there." It's very important to remember that this sense of being an individual is a *development*.[19] We are not born with it. The more parents and others reinforce a child's separateness or specialness, the more the child will develop habits that draw strong lines around the belief "I am different from others" or "I am better than others" or "I will be famous someday." In some societies, such as many in Asia, children are strongly encouraged to identify themselves with their families, their community, or even their society, rather than with only their individual identity.[20] Nothing is lost in autonomy by having an identity that joins with others, as long as children develop the necessary capacities for decision making and self-governance.

A Human Identity

Between age three and six or seven years, children go on to shape capacities that allow them to comprehend what we call reality: time, space, and causal connections (for example, when you do this, that happens). The child now joins the adult world of "yesterday, today, tomorrow" and "the sky is up but the ground is down." At first these new perspectives are wobbly, but they mature and become reliable. These new frames of reference, as Jean Piaget and his followers show, permit all children to develop a "practical intelligence." After six or seven, children can usually get around in the adult world of reality on a fairly reliable basis.[21] This is why the age of seven was originally understood as the first age of reason and responsibility in a child's life.[22]

An extremely important aspect of this early development is the mastery of language—talking to ourselves and others—in regard to our own actions.[23] The first stories children love to tell and be told are about themselves or other children. Most of all, they love to hear stories of children's actions—what children do and how they change things. They like to rehearse and express the feelings of being a mover and a shaker. This kind of imagination and imaginative play is key to a child's budding autonomy. "I can make something happen" continues to be highly motivating for all of us, even as our desires become more future-oriented and complex.

Encouraging children to play among themselves and make use of imagination (for example, using ordinary household objects as boats and trains and swords, or playing house) is more important than special lessons or specific educational toys in this period of life.[24] In fact apart from learning basic scholarship at school and learning to swim or other instructions for safety, children are best left free of elaborate lessons until they are about ten or eleven years old, when a new kind of identity begins to develop. Young children need to exercise imagination in active play with one another in order to practice the basic skills of autonomy and cooperation more than they need highly specialized instructions.

Moral training is the exception to this. As you saw in the last chapter, our capacities for virtue and good character begin to take shape even in early childhood. Children are readily guided by stories and examples before the age of eleven. First they need to learn the rules for becoming a good human being—to cherish their lives and the lives of others, to tell the truth, to take only what is given and not the things of others. Then they need to practice these rules regularly in sharing and cooperating with others, especially peers. Respecting the rules is surely viewed differently by a child when a parent is watching (the parent has power) than when a child is playing with a peer (who is an equal). Mastering the requirements of becoming a good human being takes knowledge and practice with parents and peers for a growing child to figure out what the rules mean and why they are taught.

In order eventually to become wholly empathic with other humans, we must first truly master the cognitive and affective distinctions between the three great classes of beings: objects, animals, and persons.[25] After all, a human being is a physical object and an animal. If you drop a person out of a window, the body will fall like any other object, according to the laws of gravity. It's also possible to treat a person like an animal; the original invention of behavioral psychology, for instance, was based on the premise that people respond to reinforcements and punishment, just as animals do. And yet human beings have self-conscious emotions, abstract reasoning, and complex subjective lives, which makes them quite different from any other animal. Understanding and feeling what it means to be a person is critical to a full range of human empathy and conscience.

Children, teens, and young adults may feel a trust and respect for their pets and other animals that they cannot readily feel for people, members of their own species. If this empathic preference for pets remains in adulthood, it is a sign that emotional, moral, and ethical development has been stunted. Even Robert Tulloch and James Parker cherished their pets and loved animals. I believe they would not have been able to kill a dog. They would have felt too much empathy for the dog. In order to connect with their humanity, adolescents and adults have to fully identify with being human.

To do so, they must have respect for the ubiquity of human suffering, some knowledge of the range of human emotions, and a basic understanding of the ways in which human families and groups develop through their relationships and interdependence. How did earlier generations attain all this before the invention of psychology? Through sustained cooperation in activities—such as farming, having a family business, running a household—that everyone engaged in and depended on. Parents acted as leaders in these activities and taught their children how to behave. Children witnessed people of all ages and status working together. Cooperation and respect for elders were required for the survival of the group. These depended on and were enhanced by moral education.

In this period of time, we have to retrieve our compass for moral education, first teaching rules for humane, civil conduct and then making sure that children engage in countless situations in which these rules translate into the smooth functioning of the group and its hierarchy. Being and feeling ordinary assists children and adults in both morality and autonomy. When we're ordinary human beings, we can accept life's disappointments and difficulties with an appreciation for what they can teach us. We know how to function both as a responsible group member and as a leader, to be emotionally intelligent about our impulses and needs, and to be compassionate about the demands that life makes on all of us.

As a parent, you should take advantage of your child's participation on teams or in other groups to ask her questions about her emotional self-awareness and her empathy with others. Whether she is holding the flag at the start of the school day or is the soccer captain, these are occasions when she can appreciate how others provide the platform or opportunity for her to fill a role that corresponds to their needs as well as her own.

Your own example of leadership in your family should model these same principles via a willingness to be transparent about your feelings and about your reliance on others, although not as an equal with your child, and in terms she can understand. Your leadership style—your role as an authority—is crucial in helping her develop autonomy and good character. Be a leader in her presence and talk to her about how you make decisions and what is most important to you when you're making decisions that involve your own or others' welfare. Oddly enough, embracing our interdependence makes it easier to practice self-determination and autonomy. Being ordinary allows us to tap into the richness of our shared humanity.

CHAPTER SIX

The Value of Being Ordinary

A decade and a half ago, when my children were teenagers, high grades and "giftedness" were less emphasized as the keys to happiness and success than they now are.[1] My children didn't make all A's, nor did I think it was vitally important that they do so. Since they are successful in their careers now, I can see that their grades in high school, and even college, didn't end up mattering all that much.

Too much parental praise for grades, appearance, thinness, wit, and athletic or musical performance interferes with a child's feeling ordinary and in fact can interrupt the development of self-determination by creating an intense hunger for admiration or approval from others, as we have seen. Feeding our children "junk praise" is similar to feeding them junk food that spawns unhealthy cravings. Under these conditions, a person cannot easily learn from experience, as Andrew so poignantly showed us in the last chapter.

What parents and other elders repeatedly say about the individual identity of a young child will have a lasting effect. Young children (under ten or eleven) believe what they hear their elders say about them because these youngsters lack an inner skeptic who says, "Why is she saying that?" or "I don't think I can measure up to that." As I said earlier, a child of six or seven wakes up to an individual identity. That first identity—"That's me, I'm golden" or "I'm smart" or "I'm special" or "I'm important"— accrues largely from what parents and teachers and older siblings have said, or even more important, implied, about the child. These are the stories that children tell themselves about "me." Unintentionally, I'm Okay–You're Okay parents may convey or engender in a child a self-importance or superiority that later leads to a self-esteem trap, interfering with the maturing of autonomy, morality, and identification with community and family.

Being Gifted

I visited Dr. Marlene Maron in her office at a psychological services department.[2] I wanted to speak with Dr. Maron because many families—middle class and working class—pass through her offices in search of help. Marlene is a youthful-looking midlife woman with soft dark curls, a warm smile, and wire-framed glasses. She quickly opened up about the changes she's seeing. "I'm seeing more self-importance and more arrogance in middle-class and upper-middle-class children. I'm intrigued by it, why it's happening. I think it may be because we feel our children are so special." She contrasts this with what she's observed in less highly educated parents. "Working-class parents seem to have a more no-nonsense style, even though they too cherish their children. For example, I carpooled a little boy to music camp with my daughter. After the first day the boy cried and said, 'It's too hard at the camp. I don't want to go back.' His mother didn't even consider that. Whereas I might say, 'Well, it's important to finish what you've started' or 'It's really going to be fun to learn these things,' his mother said, 'We paid $215 and you're going to see this through. It might be hard, but you will deal.' And he did. He worked hard and did well." Marlene believes that many parents like herself, middle-class and highly educated, don't want to be "unpopular" with their children. They don't want to be authority figures, to set limits and enforce rules.

What particularly interested Dr. Maron, though, was how to deal with specialness in children who are truly gifted, performing better than others academically, musically, or athletically. She spoke about her eight-year-old son, whom she described as a very bright boy who seems aware of his intelligence without grandiosity. "My son is really bright. He knows he's really bright, but I don't think he's grandiose about it. He's just realistically aware that he can do things that other kids can't do. He's not a show-off, but he tells me that he's well aware of these differences. I'm always struggling with how to appreciate that in him without overvaluing it."

Like other high-achieving young children, Marlene's son will need to follow Peterson and Seligman's ten-year rule of persistence in mastering a discipline, to develop the capacity for emotional intelligence in leading others, and to become adept at making realistic use of negative feedback if his gifts are to lead to successful achievements as an adult. Unfortunately many parents of gifted children tend to think in terms of enhancing their gifts rather than enhancing their relational skills and virtues. While many children are bright and capable, only a handful have such great talents as to automatically command respect and recognition within a field. Instead most will need to be diligent, engage cooperatively with elders and peers, lead others, and make good decisions along the way if they are to become successful.[3]

Study upon study shows that people who have good relationships are the happiest and most successful in life.[4] To be a leader in any field, a person needs to be an active member of groups, maintain good relations within those groups, and organize others to get things done. No matter what gifts children have, they must be able to lead others with at least a modicum of emotional intelligence in order to realize their talents. Emotionally intelligent leadership is defined as realistic self-awareness (knowing your strengths and weaknesses) and self-management (knowing how to work skillfully with your own emotions in groups), as well as accurate empathy with others.[5] If special attention and opportunities are repeatedly presented to a child in a way that signals "you are better than others," this can interfere with developing the emotional intelligence he will need to get ahead in his field. As we've seen, self-importance and entitlement can become major impediments to autonomy and success whether a person has outstanding talents or not.

Recently a series of studies has also established self-compassion as a component of emotional intelligence that may be even more relevant than good self-esteem in developing talents and skills. Self-compassion includes three components: being kind and understanding toward oneself, rather than self-critical (self-kindness); viewing one's negative experiences as a normal part of the human condition (being ordinary, as I've called it here); and having mindful equanimity rather than overidentifying with painful thoughts and feelings (mindful acceptance).[6] Self-compassion allows people to work through obstacles and accept limitations that might otherwise prevent their ongoing commitment to an endeavor or relationship. Cultivating emotional intelligence and self-compassion in children includes helping them appreciate the variety of abilities and skills that support a human community.

Because of childish egocentrism, it can seem to a bright child as though he "knows everything," but parents and teachers have many opportunities to show children how their intelligence extends only to certain topics or activities. I, for instance, remember being startled at the intelligence needed to repair a car, something I saw my cousins doing even though they didn't have a high school education. I might have been a straight-A student, but I was entirely incapable of understanding a motor or repairing an automobile. Today's trends seem to go in another direction, though: pushing children to develop only the things they are good at.

As Marlene Maron warned, "In some circles, educators are really pushing children to skip grades and get special attention for their gifts. For instance, I've heard an argument that supports placing gifted children with their intellectual peers, if necessary, ahead of their chronological peers. That view holds that acceleration leads to positive outcomes for intellectually gifted kids and challenges the perspective that there are social costs to removing those children from their chronological peers. I find this movement frightening for some children; generally I don't think it's developmentally healthy for young children to be pushed to move ahead of their peers." [7] Requiring intellectually precocious kids to master the emotional and social demands of older children may not serve them well, particularly in the teenage years.

Gifted and At Risk

I very much agree with Dr. Maron, but many parents whose children are bright and doing very well in school, or outside school in music, athletics, or art, want something special to promote those gifts. Sadly they are unaware of the role of emotional intelligence and self-compassion in being successful. In 2005 the *New York Times Magazine* ran a long story entitled "Can Genius Really Be Cultivated?"[8] In addition to covering gifted-child advocates and the expensive programs they sponsor, the author, Ann Hulbert, reviewed the findings of a number of longitudinal studies that show childhood genius is not a very good predictor of adult achievement. In fact many of us know stories about creative inventors such as Thomas Edison and scientists like Albert Einstein who did not show any precocity as children. The writer Malcolm Gladwell, as noted in the article, has recently cautioned that precocity in general doesn't forecast exceptional adult performance.

I believe that the interpersonal and psychological ingredients that go into self-confidence, autonomy, self-compassion, and emotional intelligence mature slowly over time in an atmosphere of collaboration with others. Without these, special gifts can become a burden. They set children apart from others. Sometimes the story of "special" can just be too much for a child to bear — or more likely, too much for an adolescent to bear.

In 2006 the *New Yorker* magazine ran a tragic story about a fourteen-year-old gifted child who killed himself with a single shot to the head from a .22 caliber rifle.[9] Brandenn Bremmer was known as a child prodigy by almost everybody near and around the area of Nebraska where he grew up. He was handsome and talented and apparently extremely charming, and could not have been more loved by his parents, Patti and Martin. At the recommendation of a number of specialists, Brandenn's IQ was tested and retested. Once he was identified as gifted, he was placed in an array of programs that provide special experiences for children with high IQs. Pushed ahead in school (skipping grades five through eight), Brandenn was enrolled in both high school and some college courses when he killed himself.

After his death it became apparent that Brandenn had encountered some disappointments in music instruction at Colorado State University and in biology at Mid-Plains Community College. Close to the day he shot himself, Brandenn e-mailed a friend, another gifted teen, who had been asking about an earlier statement of his, "I've been depressed beyond all reason." She wanted to know what the depression was about, because, as she said, "trust me, I've been there, done that." Brandenn responded:

> *I don't know why I'm so depressed, before it was every now and then, and you know, it was just "bummed out" depressed. But now it's constant and it's just "What's the point of living anymore?" I don't know, maybe I just don't spend enough time around good friends like you. But like I can. Not out here in the middle of nowhere. At least there's this family kind of near by that aren't "Cowboys," or else just plain idiots, that I can spend time with.*[10]

Unfortunately Brandenn felt his identity as "better than" others. He worried about finding the connections he needed in his isolated rural setting, and he couldn't imagine that most people could connect to him anyway. But after some time of being in the world with a modicum of empathy, most of us discover there are no "plain idiots" to be found (or that every one of us is a plain idiot). Human beings all have strengths and weaknesses. What distinguishes people in the long run are character and virtue, not particular gifts. So when adolescent children, in the full bloom of self-consciousness and burdened with the weight of being "special," wake up to what seems to be expected by those who have idealized them, while at the same time acutely feeling their need for friendships and community, they may feel isolated, even terrified.

Children under ten cannot really question a talked-about identity. If before we even have our own view of ourselves, we repeatedly hear or surmise, "You are so special," "You're so smart," or "You're better than others," we will meet this assumption when the superego matures in later adolescence. Then, like so many of the young adults whom I've introduced in this book, we come to believe that we are or should be superior to others, and this belief becomes an obstacle and a cause of negative self-evaluation when we confront the ordinary adversities of life and our fears of humiliation and defeat.

Not until adolescence do we have the possibility of a point of view that fully permits us to see and feel ourselves in comparison with others. From the outside, the young child seems to adults to be freer and more creative than a self-conscious teenager. But on the inside, the young child has no option but to be a naive consumer of talked-about identity. Emotional and physical dependency, as well as yet-to-mature cognitive development, keeps young children close to parents' ideals, shame, fantasies, and grandiosity. For the rest of their lives, their first talked-about identity will be a ghost in the wings, if not an actor onstage. If they end up too special and different, they'll be burdened by obsessive self-focus, restless dissatisfaction, pressures to be exceptional, unreadiness to take on adult responsibilities, feelings of superiority (or inferiority), and excessive fears of being humiliated.

Caring parents will want to convey to preadolescent children—especially those with exceptional gifts or talents with words, numbers, athletics, machines, or animals—that the key to happiness is in being a *member* of the human community, an ordinary person.[11] The mirror we offer to a young child's self should reflect the importance of interdependence and sharing before that child meets the painfully self-conscious teen years.

All of a child's skills should be nurtured in an environment in which the help and capacities of others are as much appreciated as the child's. Talented students should, of course, be encouraged to reach out to tutor and help others or join teams that work together to meet challenges, but even more important, they should be expected and reminded to express gratitude to those with greater expertise on whom they depend. Requiring children to perform chores and daily activities that are serious and important to family life (like preparing meals and working on the family budget or repairing tools and machines) will inspire humility as they discover that they don't, in fact, know everything. When you are speaking about your child's accomplishments in his presence and in the presence of others, remember our interdependence. Rather than boasting about his star quality, describe how he worked together with others to accomplish his goals, and point out the strengths of those others as well. Making your child the center of attention, even when he is not present, brings a self-consciousness (to you or him) that will interfere with happiness. Celebrating success and achievement should express gratitude for what has made it possible, including your child's efforts. Similarly, when a teenager is begging for compliments, try out some of the old wisdom of deemphasizing individual beauty ("Beauty is as beauty does"), talent ("You're talented and you'll have to work hard and cooperate with lots of people to make your talent count"), or intelligence ("There are a lot of smart people in the world, and you're one of them, but that doesn't count for a lot by itself"). Mostly, make it clear to your child that these abilities are gifts that need to be given back to society and humanity in order to become truly worthwhile. Insisting that children be honest and transparent, as well as charitable in what they say about others' faults, will remind them that their words are powerful and that everyone should be spoken about and to with respect and kindness. The possibilities for refining a young child's awareness of others are endless and can be tailored to each child's abilities and situation. Perhaps most important is teaching a child through experience—working side by side with elders on group endeavors—that mastery and success are not easily accomplished but require a long process, a lot of honesty and insight, and a great deal of investment from others. In a child's earliest years, as we'll see, parents must lay a secure foundation for good character and compassion (for self and other) in their children.

Self-Consciousness and the Superego

Whatever identity a child inherits from early childhood—special, defective, ordinary—he will justify, argue with, rationalize, promote, and react to when he takes an overview of himself for the rest of his life. Of Andrew's early life identification with being an artist, his therapist wrote, "He wanted to be the kind of painter who formulated unusual ideas about the visual world. But as soon as he began to suspect that he might not be sufficiently gifted to achieve this, he would give up painting in despair. He would turn to something else, only to resume his obsessive preoccupation with painting as soon as the 'imperfection' of the new work became intolerable." [12] Instead of enjoying the talents he had and working with his strengths and weaknesses in order to master the field, Andrew despaired of ever being the painter that he felt he should be. Through his therapy Andrew became more flexible in response to the demands for perfection that came from his grandiose ideals. He moved his special self away from center stage and into the wings.

When we are about eighteen months old, the birth of our ego (the function that allows us to guide ourselves and maintain an identity over time) is announced by the onset of the self-conscious emotions, those emotions that motivate us to compare ourselves with others and to feel separate from them.[13] You may not know much about the formal aspects of your emotions, but you certainly know what it feels like to be overwhelmed with emotion and taken aback by a flood of images and body sensations that throw you off-center and motivate you to do things, to react.

From neuroscience and psychological research on the emotions, we know that the human infant is initially equipped with "primary emotions," which are sorted by researchers into five or seven flavors. I prefer the simplicity of five: joy, curiosity, sadness, aversion (or disgust), and fear.[14]

Often when clients in therapy don't know what they are feeling, they review the pop-psychology list of "mad, sad, glad, scared, or turned off," but can't seem to locate their experience in any one of them. They would do well instead to look among the self-conscious emotions. Many of us do not know that the self-conscious emotions make serious demands on our identity and autonomy.

If you think about how you feel when you imagine yourself in comparison with others, you could probably name almost all the self-conscious emotions: embarrassment, guilt, pride, shame, jealousy, envy, and self-pity are the main ones.[15] Our notorious human prefrontal cortex, the outcrop of brain that grows roughly just behind our forehead, equips us with motivations and sensations that other animals don't have. Even if other animals are somewhat conscious of themselves, it's unlikely that they have complex, abstract, and sustained consciousness of themselves. We humans compare ourselves with others, both in our imagination and in the immediate presence of others. Elephants and ants don't do that. Of course we are also motivated by the primary emotions, which we share with most other animals. Getting stuck in self-consciousness, however, puts us at risk for developing a special self and other identity problems that throw us off the axis of our being. In order to refine the inner voice that can guide us, we have to cultivate a gentle, mindful self-acceptance (attempting to override self-consciousness) that permits us to see ourselves realistically in the context of others who help us and compete with us.

The self-conscious emotions interfere with this kind of equanimity. They focus our attention urgently on the self and away from whatever else is happening—and of course something else is always happening. Our self-conscious feelings preoccupy us with anxiety about the self. Whatever we feel about the self at any moment—pride or guilt or shame—will take center stage and block out other experiences and perceptions.

The birth of self-consciousness is called the terrible two's or the power struggle of toddlerhood because the human infant becomes acutely aware of "I'm in here. I want/don't want this or that." [16] The toddler suddenly expresses a will, a separateness, and an in-here-ness that did not previously exist. Self-consciousness is necessary for human autonomy because of the complexity of the human brain and its interactions. The self-conscious emotions will eventually allow us to take a view from the balcony, that reflective overview of identity, actions, and speech. Many diverse perceptions and reactions are going on moment to moment in the adult brain. The self-conscious emotions trigger self-awareness that helps us answer the question "What's going on here?" This self function allows us to make choices, to review preferences, and eventually to look back into the past and forward into the future. These are skills that are required for mature and autonomous decision making.

The very first marker on the path to mature autonomy is the

toddler's ability to manage her impulses and actions. Self-consciousness helps with that. "Oh, I can do this. I can stop myself from hitting my brother." When young children can confidently manage their impulses, they are able to relate to others more enthusiastically and move about more independently in the physical environment. Civilized behavior is usually expected by the age of six or seven.

Then the next developmental milestone emerges. Mastering a human sense of time, space, and causality, as I said earlier, initiates a whole new dimension of self-consciousness. A personal story with a past and a future begins to develop, alongside clearer preferences.[17] "I know I like chocolate ice cream, and so the next time we go to Ben and Jerry's, I'll ask for chocolate." At this point children can follow rules for character development on their own because they can feel shame, guilt, and remorse, as well as recognize the consequences of their actions. Of course it takes a long time for children to refine the meanings that link their intentions and their actions with the effects on others of their behaviors.

At about the age of eleven or twelve, children encounter the final revolution of self-consciousness: the birth of the superego and the eruption of self-reflective awareness.[18] This milestone depends on certain cortical connections and other neural events that start developing in early adolescence and don't finish until young adulthood. When these capacities have matured, young adults have the potential for, but not the guarantee of, human empathy: the ability to step into others' shoes to infer what their experience might be like. The full flowering of human empathy, as I have stressed throughout, depends on many relational skills that are practiced especially through cooperation and sharing in a family or group in which one knows both more and less than other members.[19]

All good parents idealize their children, at least during infancy and often until adolescence. We cannot help but shine the golden glow of parental pride on what our children do well, how beautiful they are, and what unique talents they bring to the world. And yet if parents or other adults persist in implying or saying that a child is extraordinary, special, or golden in a way that sets the child apart from others, then that child will be at risk for developing the symptoms of the self-esteem trap.

Repeatedly we've seen how exaggerated praise sows the seeds of a special self, but there is another path to self-inflation—compensation for feeling inferior.[20] When a child infers or is told over time by a parent, elder, or older sibling that he is inferior (stupid, mediocre, ugly), that child may either identify with or oppose that message when he gets into adolescence. If the child identifies with being inferior, he will frequently feel shame and envy, believing that he does not have the inner resources that others have. Psychotherapy or other kinds of help can correct this, allowing a grown child to combat such "internalized inferiority" and develop a realistic perception of his strengths and weaknesses. If, on the other hand, an adolescent or young adult opposes internalized inferiority by compensating with an exaggerated self-importance, then she might sound like a child who was overpraised. For example she might say something like, "By the time I'm forty, I'll retire, because I'm not just going to become a hairdresser, I'm going to start my own chain of hair salons and I'll be a millionaire." Ironically, then, some people who grow up with unfair attacks on their identity have the same kind of special self that belongs to someone who was indulged in childhood.

If there are a lot of distortions (either positive or negative) in our original identities, we develop a corrupt lens for seeing ourselves.[21] Our view from the balcony will be blocked or clouded and we won't know why. Maybe we will believe that our talents are greater than they are, as Andrew did in his artwork, and then feel deeply ashamed when we are exposed for being less exceptional than we thought. We may mistakenly believe in our inferiority and compensate through other beliefs. If our parents were afraid to act as authority figures, we may be left with a premature belief in the excellence of our own judgments and overstep boundaries with those who are more experienced — only to feel ashamed and defeated when we are criticized for it.

Professor Gigi Marks, of Ithaca College, recognizes that many young people feel shame about their appearance and bodies, leading to sexual acting out. She says, "There's such a glorification of the body and pornography in a way that is, on the one hand, accessible to everyone on the Internet and, on the other hand, never accessible. It's fantasy. The pressure and expectation to look young and slim are so strong that young people don't have any realistic image of their bodies." Reflecting back on her own struggles with perfection, Gigi Marks recalls, "About ten years ago, I was just getting together with my partner, who is a very good athlete. I was okay, but I wasn't great at cross-country skiing, which we did together. I was in counseling at this time, and when I brought up this topic, my counselor said directly to me, 'Hey, it's okay to be mediocre at this. You're good at other things.' This statement was a clear and profound permission to be ordinary. It was freeing." The permission to be ordinary, to have some failures and mistakes and not know in advance how to do things, is missing in many young adults today.

The best remedy for a special self is equanimity in the face of desires for praise, success, or power. To find that matter-of-fact realistic view from our balcony, we need a gentle, objective awareness when we overview ourselves. No matter our stage in life, we can improve our equanimity by embracing a fundamentally human identity and learn how to function optimally in the relationships on which we depend.

Practice Being Ordinary

Our experience of a human self is in a constant state of flux. We are profoundly influenced from moment to moment by other people, the environment, and internal factors. If we believe that we are set apart from others (either superior or inferior) and that we have to protect ourselves from their influence, we cannot become autonomous or emotionally intelligent. We make the wrong decisions or feel unable to make choices at all. Whether we are preoccupied with positive or negative feelings about ourselves, when we are distracted by self-consciousness, we cannot pay close attention to whatever else is going on; we can't read others' signals well, and we can't be really effective as leaders or members of groups.[22]

When we find ourselves in such circumstances, what can we do? For some of us, like Andrew, psychotherapy is a place to begin to move our self-obsession and restless dissatisfaction off center stage. Whether or not you are in psychotherapy, though, if you follow the six simple practices that I describe below, you can cultivate emotional intelligence, autonomy, and compassion for self and others—in both yourself and your children—in a way that highlights our common humanity and ordinariness.

These practices were traditionally a part of child rearing and family life in our society, but they have dropped away in this era of being special. They can be taught to children and practiced by adults. With younger children you have to convey these ideas through examples and stories as well as guidance. Once a child is around seven years old, though, you can help him memorize the six practices and what they mean, along with other rules for moral conduct, such as the Ten Commandments. Refer to these practices and rules frequently when you're talking together, as at family meals. Although they overlap with some of the virtues that I talked about in chapter four, they should be viewed as exercises or activities rather than values or attitudes.

They go by slightly different names in different religious traditions, but I like the following:

1. Generosity

2. Discipline

3. Patience

4. Diligence

5. Concentration

6. Wisdom

When I was first taught these practices, many years ago, I was told that the order mattered. Each one is grounded on all that comes before it.[23]

Generosity, the first, is the preparation and foundation for all of the others. It is the practice of thinking about others, keeping them in mind, and giving to them. Even in our infancy, we give much of our attention and concern to our caregivers. Infants and young children want nothing more than for their caregivers to be happy, safe, and healthy. Our earliest impulse is to engage with and cheer up our mothers. We are born with the desire to make and retain attachment bonds and to keep our caregivers happy. Babies are hardwired to gaze into their mothers' eyes and delight them.

This basic impulse to give to others can be badly distorted and corrupted as a result of abuse, neglect, or trauma. It can be used for the wrong purposes and may even be seen as a weakness, but it is a fundamental impulse in all of us. The most natural way to develop the skill of generosity is to look around, at any moment, and see what can be done to help in the environment you're in. Even young children can be taught to help others by carrying things, being quiet, and stepping aside when others need this kind of attention or deference. Often people believe that generosity belongs in special circumstances, like volunteering, but that's not the case. In fact generosity—openhearted help that is given freely—is usually best cultivated in unarranged situations, a sort of "random kindness" activity. Although volunteering can increase our children's or our own generosity, it can also limit it, because we may secretly feel, "Okay, now I've helped, I've done my bit, and I don't need to be sensitive to anyone else's needs now." Alertness to what's going on at any moment, giving help where it is needed, is a long-term goal.

For teenagers and adolescents, it may be useful to volunteer and work with the poor, the aging, or some other group in need, simply to expand a teenager's horizons. But for GenMe especially, it's important to learn that helping others is not something that is scheduled according to one's own convenience. For children and teens, it's relatively easy to assist a friend but hard to help a competitor (perhaps a sibling or another rival). In family meetings, parents can motivate even their youngest children to stretch their generosity in asking them to help a rival sibling. Parents should set examples themselves, by showing kindness and generosity to their own rivals as well.

As a practice, generosity will awaken our feelings of appreciation and gratitude. When we see how empathic and compassionate we must become in order to truly help, we begin to recognize how we have been helped. It's almost automatic, then, for our hearts to fill with gratitude for what we have been given.

GenMe'ers may not feel much gratitude for all they've been given because they have not practiced generosity, especially in the form of acts of kindness for the elders and others on whom they have depended for their own lives.

Over time in adulthood, we may come to the wisdom that there is no difference between giving to another and receiving ourselves. Each gift to someone else is a pleasure for ourselves and often brings us new insight into what it means to be human. This joining of self and other through giving is another long-term aim of the practice of generosity.

Discipline, second on the list, builds from generosity, because in our efforts to help others we must become responsible and reliable. Discipline does not mean punishment here. Rather it means the training of good character (through honesty and kindness) and wise actions (through respect and compassion for self and others) so that we can come to rely on ourselves to make good decisions and be responsible. This kind of moral, ethical, and social training begins even in toddlerhood as youngsters are asked to contain their impulses, respect elders and the ill, and use proper words (not profanity, for instance) to express their needs and feelings.

Living a disciplined life starts with the regularity of a structured family or household in which certain rituals (for example, family meals and family meetings), activities, and chores are built into daily life. As I've already said, kids and teenagers should have chores that are serious and contribute to the welfare of the family or household. For example, if a child is responsible for preparing dinner one evening a week (coming up with the menu and fixing the meal), then all other family members depend on his carrying out the activity.

Discussing these kinds of tasks and setting up family rituals takes place in the weekly family meeting, in which plans are made and results are reviewed. Children need adult instruction and support to set down a daily discipline, but once the tasks and rituals are in place, children can carry through on their own. After all, in the past, children and teens worked on family farms and in family businesses, usually starting at around the age of seven. Disciplined engagement with family life leads to true self-confidence and self-worth.

Even as adults we need a rhythm and regularity for our daily activities so that we know what we are getting up to do in the morning and what time we will go to sleep at night. Each day has a meaning and a method for expressing our purpose in the world.

Patience, the third practice on the list, is enhanced by our generosity and discipline, because patience requires a mindful self-acceptance of our daily life, just as it is. Following the lead of my Buddhist teacher, Shinzen Young, I define patience as the "radical permission to feel your feelings all the way through." He connects patience with our willingness to fully experience what is taking place in our senses and our feelings *before acting.* When we do this, we don't feel rushed, even under pressure. Children can be taught to be alert to their feelings and can recognize quite easily where they are feeling them in their bodies. The practice of patience begins in childhood. Ask your child to stop and just feel or sense in the body what is happening when emotions are stirred. From time to time, take advantage of stressful moments and join your child in being quiet or still and simply experience what's happening. Patience isn't a white-knuckle holding back, but rather the practice of allowing ourselves to be fully accepting of our experience before we speak or act. The first three practices on the list provide a foundation for emotional intelligence in being members and leaders in groups, in being able to feel and manage our own reactivity while recognizing the effects others have on us.

Diligence, the fourth practice, means strong, assiduous effort. Diligence is a kind of mental muscle that we develop through doing things properly and well. Sometimes it comes now in learning sports or playing music, but traditionally it would come from doing chores properly. Doing schoolwork carefully or being generous and kind to others can also develop diligence. Diligence clearly depends on patience; if we cannot allow our own feelings simply to be, without overreacting to them, we cannot become diligent.

Concentration, the fifth practice on the list, is undergirded by generosity, discipline, patience, and diligence. Concentration is a mindful awareness that we use in doing whatever is before us, being both sharp and relaxed. When we are both attentive and matter-of-fact, we do not tire easily, because we feel refreshed and renewed through a smooth engagement of our awareness. Children are frequently asked to concentrate when they study but are rarely taught how to do so. Anyone can learn simple mindfulness practices—for example, pausing to hear completely ordinary sounds: the ringing of a phone or the chime of a clock. Or when walking through a doorway, to return your awareness to your body so that you recognize the experience of moving from one environment to another. Young children enjoy learning these practices. Concentration is the skill of patiently and gently returning our awareness to the object of our concentration. When the mind wanders, gently bring it back. If it wanders a thousand times, bring it back a thousand and one times.

Wisdom is the final practice on the list and the natural culmination of all the others. Engaging in our relationships, our work, and our play through these practices, we find that valuable insights begin to well up. Wisdom is not by any means an automatic outgrowth of increasing age or experience.[24] Growing older does not guarantee growing wiser. As I noted in the first chapter, scientific research on wisdom has shown that its seeds are planted early in life, especially in childhood, in the ways we relate to, tolerate, and learn from life's adversity. Resilience in facing discontent, pain, and difficulty, and accepting them as ordinary companions, seems to form the roots of wisdom. Developing and using all of the other practices on the list provides both openings and skills that allow us to encounter any life experience, especially painful or difficult ones, as an opportunity to learn about being human. Nothing has to be refused, because nothing seems alien or impossible. Self-compassion and compassion toward others are natural outgrowths of wisdom. And the first three practices—generosity, discipline, and patience—are the building blocks of wisdom.

All six of these practices, along with other moral training, will eventually lead to identifying with being an ordinary person, a member of the community. When a sound conscience meets up with the superego in later adolescence, an ordinary child can have the makings of wisdom, even before adult life has unfolded. As we have seen, the symptoms of a special self can block the development of a sound conscience, emotional intelligence, compassion, and wisdom. In the next chapter we will look at the role religion and spirituality can play in preventing or undoing the self-esteem trap—helping us maintain a compassionate and connected ordinary self.

CHAPTER SEVEN

Religion and Reverence

For centuries religion has played an integral role in human life. It has been the source of rules to live by, the protector of moral codes, the ultimate guide toward greater wisdom and meaning. For good and for bad, religion has provided answers to our most pressing personal questions: why we're here, what the purpose of our lives is supposed to be, why we die, and what happens afterward. Religion has also provided guidelines for raising our children in the framework of a faith that our lives are about something bigger and more meaningful than our individual identities.

Many I'm Okay–You're Okay parents left their childhood religions, as I did, because they deeply disagreed with what the religion stood for or they could no longer embrace the principles of their faith. Other post-Boomer parents were raised without formal religion because their parents were not members of a church or synagogue. The shift away from organized religion has produced some gaps in family functioning, parenting, and child development. In chapter four I addressed one of the gaps:

overlooking the importance of conscience and virtue. Here I want to talk about some others: a lack of purpose and meaning in our lives and our deaths, and the absence of a deep reverence for our existence.

When religions are alive and healthy, children grow up in a social environment that inculcates a respect for human existence. In the absence of this kind of influence, they can easily get the impression that their lives are supposed to be about them-selves—having a good time, maybe having a family, making money. Becoming famous may be the most exalted goal for a GenMe'er. Very few young people question the legitimacy, for instance, of a contemporary cultural icon like Paris Hilton, who is famous mostly for being famous. But her fame would have been impossible four decades ago. Back then you believed that your life was not yours to squander. Paris Hilton wouldn't have made any sense. If in the short space of a human lifetime, your life needs to make sense to God, as it would have had to in the past, then your search becomes a serious business. Fame for the sake of fame just doesn't compute.

In the twenty-first century, helping the young find a purpose and develop reverence largely falls to educational, cultural, and family institutions that are not imbued with religious meanings. Many debates ensue about how to teach or inculcate these kinds of larger values. To a great extent, educated people may hope that science will settle the debates. Although science in its many forms may be thought to replace religion for the educated, the aims and practices of science are only distorted if we demand that they provide the kind of personal meaning and guidance that have traditionally come from religion.

While I have great respect for science and scientific research, and draw liberally on it in all of the work I do, I regard science as more a method of investigation than a set of guiding principles. Indeed I believe we have to go beyond science and connect with a deeper meaning in our own experience—something that used to be called the divine—in order to get a view of our lives that transcends our separate identities. For this reason I want to talk about religion and reverence instead of spirituality.

When I said at the beginning of the book that getting the right tone was important and challenging, I didn't have this particular chapter in mind, but I should have. Religion, however we approach it at this moment in time, is an excruciatingly sensitive subject. In advance of saying what I have to say about its role in understanding ourselves and helping us raise our children, I ask for your patience. I hope that I can persuade you to take a fresh look at the issues I introduce. Some of you may have long rejected religion, especially in its organized forms, because of the harm it has brought both to individuals and to the world. Others of you may embrace religion for a variety of reasons that have everything or nothing to do with faith. Problematically religions have notoriously held up their ideals in such a way that some people feel they must measure themselves and judge others by standards that undermine our common humanity. If religion intentionally or unintentionally enlarges our egotism and undermines our compassion and connection, it leads to destructive outcomes. Wanting to avoid these outcomes while embracing the essence of religion, some of you may have turned toward spirituality or an "individual" religion that picks and chooses from hundreds of years of diverse traditions.

Instead of following the popular trend of talking about spirituality, though, I want to focus on religion and a religious attitude. I regard religion as more foundational and serious than spirituality. And I've found among GenMe young adults and teens a reticence to engage in serious inquiry about transcendental questions, although they have a lot of interest in, and involvement with, mythic and fictional supernatural themes in popular media. I'm Okay–You're Okay parents have asked me repeatedly in therapy and in public lectures how they should introduce their children to the deeper meaning of life. This chapter is my answer.

The Role of Religion: Then and Now

Let me begin with a little background. Up until the 1970s most of us grew up in a religion.[1] We went to church or temple regularly with our parents. Neighborhoods were often built around churches and synagogues (instead of shopping malls), and many social events took place in them. Religion was an expected part of life.

Consider the Broll family as a typical example of religious family life in the midtwentieth century. Doris and John Broll met in the military during the 1950s and despite being from different geographical areas (a farm boy from Texas and a city girl from the East Coast), discovered they had much in common in their shared Catholic upbringing. They married and rapidly had three children: Stephen, Mary, and David. The Brolls bought a new home in a housing development of ranch houses and settled down to raising their family. Doris stayed home, of course, to care for the children.

Every Sunday the family attended 7 AM Mass and then went out to breakfast together. The two sons became altar boys. All three children attended classes in religious training and were confirmed at the age of fourteen. The Brolls' story could just as easily be Jewish as Christian. It was the rule rather than the exception.

Today the three adult Broll children are married, with children of their own. Stephen, the oldest, left the Catholic Church in his midtwenties and is exploring Judaism. Mary left the church during her college years and has no religious affiliation. David attends Mass every Sunday, while his daughter and wife go to the Unitarian church.

All three grown-up Broll children acknowledge the huge impact that religion played in their lives: impressing them with the need to do the right thing, the feeling that their actions ultimately mattered, and the belief that they are connected to all of humanity, as well as to a deeper source. They also struggle against the negative aftereffects of their childhood religion: guilt, fear, conflicts with the church doctrines on sexuality and social policies. Even though the Broll children rebelled against their religion, they say that it stays with them, means a lot to them, is a part of their identities forever. Despite the fact that the only time they have attended Catholic church together in the past twenty years was for their mother's funeral, they value being Catholic as part of who they are.

Not so for their own kids. Their own sons and daughters, the next generation, were rarely brought to church as children and now have no use for Catholicism. At a time when God's name is more associated with politics, war, and sexual scandal than with church potlucks, they have grown up in an altogether different religious climate. As a result they have none of the "Catholic guilt" that still afflicts their parents. Nor do they have a tradition that upholds the concepts of truth, love, service, faith, hope, beauty, and ritual. This is true for many of today's young adults. For them the concept of religion is alien.

An American man, a good friend of mine, who has spent the past thirty-seven years living in several Zen temples in Japan (he's a Zen monk), recently visited the States. "I noticed," he told me, "that the children of my evangelical Christian family members have turned out better than the children of my counterculture friends. I have often wondered if it's because of their religion." Yes, probably at least in part. It's likely that the children of his counterculture friends were also raised in an environment of I'm Okay–You're Okay parenting, caught in the self-esteem trap. Cultivating good character and a sound conscience in our children can take place outside of religious influence, as we have seen, but it may happen more smoothly and easily under the influence of religion, provided that religion is alive and meaningful to the parents.

Why We Need Religion

Wanting to find out what is real on a deeper level is the best reason to turn to religion. Like science, religion answers questions about the powers, meaning, and connections that underpin our lives, focusing especially on moral, ethical, relational, and existential issues. Religious practices over the ages have given people the opportunity to explore the depths of their spirituality and humanity—to understand what it means to love, to be of service, to know the truth, and to sustain hope amid the adversity and misery of life. For me as a child, church was the only place that I truly felt the effects of art, music, and ritual on my little being. The excitement of participating in the drama of ceremony—with incense and stained glass and gorgeous vases of flowers on the altar—stayed with me a great deal more than the words that were spoken. Church was a place apart from all of the other places I lived. I often found myself going into reverie there, contemplating the mysteries of life. Today too few young adults have a sanctuary in which to cultivate their engagement with the mysteries of life. Where do they go to have a time and place apart from busyness?

In the early 1980s I first read the lectures on religion and psychology given by the psychoanalyst Carl Jung in 1937 at Yale

University. In these lectures Jung shows why religious seeking is a natural condition of human beings. He asks the question "What is the original religious experience?" and answers by expanding on the definition of the Latin root *religio:*

> *a careful consideration and observation of certain dynamic factors, understood to be "powers," spirits, demons, gods, laws, ideas, ideals, or whatever name man has given to such factors as he has found in his world powerful, dangerous . . . or helpful enough to be taken into careful consideration, or grand, beautiful . . . and meaningful enough to be devoutly adored and loved.*[2]

Jung's definition is inclusive, encompassing any practice that stems from awe, and to which we give careful consideration and study—anything grand and beautiful that we take seriously.

I want to make clear that by using the term "religion," I do not mean a creed or even an organization of people. Rather I mean a careful and serious attitude about matters of transcendence. By transcendence I mean those feelings and experiences that break through the limits of our personal self and identity, conveying a connection to the source of our being. Religions give various names to this source: God, Truth, Allah, Tao, True Self, and Buddha Mind are a few of them. A religious attitude, enhanced through beliefs and practices, keeps us in touch with a perplexity and a reverence as we come to recognize that our lives and deaths follow natural spiritual laws. When your religion is real it connects you to a shared experience of the source of your being that has been described and validated by human beings over eons of time. Some spiritual and religious practices fail to do this and instead promise special favors and personal gains for individuals.

Some types of New Age spirituality, for example, misleadingly promise people that they can become famous, powerful, or safe just by saying a mantra, a prayer, or an affirmation. Naturally this is much easier than cultivating good character, virtues, and reverence. And it's also easier than leading a disciplined life that includes lengthy periods of meditation or prayer. Some types of contemporary spirituality may even encourage you to believe that you have a special status or an "inside channel" that can be used just for your own purposes.[3] True spiritual practices are not for personal gain, but renew our sense of connection to one another and to something that goes beyond our own identity.

Along these lines I heard a wonderful little story about Mother Teresa that illustrates my point about spiritual power. A Catholic priest who is a friend of mine was on sabbatical at the Vatican in Rome, and he was to have an audience with the Pope. Apparently, in going for an audience with the Pope you take a number as you would waiting in line at a bakery or deli. Astonishingly, his number happened to be next to Mother Teresa's number. And so they sat side by side for some time, and he asked her a lot of questions about what it was like to be Mother Teresa. She answered kindly and patiently, and when my friend's number was called, she did something that is not at all unusual in the Catholic tradition: she knelt before him and asked for his blessing. As a priest, he was empowered to give such a blessing, whereas she was not.

My friend was flabbergasted, looking down at Mother Teresa kneeling at his feet. "I thought, how could I, being the neurotic and sometimes mistaken person that I am, give my blessing to Mother Teresa? While I was lost in self-consciousness, she looked up at me and said, 'It's not about you personally, Father!'" The power we tap into spiritually is not about us personally. Rather it is the power to connect to a source that goes beyond our limited identity and should not be confused with our ego.

Buddhism in My Life

When I turned away from my childhood religion because I could no longer believe it, I began a serious investigation into the world's religions, studying and attending different traditions. I wanted to belong to a community in which I could discover and practice methods of making a deeper connection to my own experience than I could get in secular settings. After a couple of years of searching, I landed in the Rochester Zen Center in Rochester, New York. Zen suited me well because it didn't compromise my intellect and was grounded in practical reality; it was what I was searching for. I took formal vows in 1971 and began a long journey that has had transformative effects and impacts on my life ever since.

Similar to the adult children of Doris and John Broll, my children have had their individual responses to my religion. One has a regular practice of Zen right now, and another is a student of Yoga and has recently also become a Buddhist, not in a Zen sect. Our oldest child, now married, is skeptical about religion and doesn't affiliate with any. When they were growing up, there were many times when our children felt annoyed and self-conscious about our beliefs and practices, but that was temporary.

When my daughter was graduating from high school, more than a decade ago, I overheard a conversation she was having with her friends. A friend said something about having grown up without any religious education, and my daughter responded, "Oh, wow, our house was really different! We talked about religious and spiritual topics all the time!" I was a little surprised, because I was afraid that my approach hadn't been formal enough, that I hadn't conveyed the true value of Buddhism, which can be a hard religion for children to understand. What I gleaned from her comment, though, was that the seriousness of the conviction that my husband and I expressed, as well as our emphasis on good character and virtue, had had real impact. When I sit down with my grown children now, they are neither too cynical nor too casual about the short ceremonies (such as meal prayers) that we may ask them to participate in. They respect our devotions.

Finding Out What's Real

I have heard countless parents say, "Even though I don't really believe, I take my children to church or synagogue. When they're grown up, they can decide for themselves whether or not they want to practice." Although the parents are well meaning, hoping to bring in positive effects of religious training, they are setting up their children for spiritual cynicism: a jaded attitude about religion. As we saw in the last two chapters, teens wake up to the identity they've internalized from childhood and ask themselves, "Who am I?" When they answer, "Catholic" — or "Methodist" or "Jewish" or "Muslim" — they will check out how that identity feels. If their identity does not correspond to something real, they are likely to feel anger at being duped, and they may even assume that all spiritual pursuits are empty of true meaning. Adolescents (and sometimes children) readily pick up on whether the adults around them actually believe what they profess. So when it comes to introducing religion into your own or your children's life, here's a caveat: Don't pretend. If you pretend, you and your children may lose out on a great opportunity.

You may recall Dr. David Hilfiker, the physician who moved from a rural life into a ghetto in order to be a part of a Christian community that serves the poor. I interviewed Dr. Hilfiker and his wife, Marja, in their apartment in the Adams-Morgan area of Washington, DC. A tall, slim, bearded man with glasses and a wry look, Dr. Hilfiker remarked, "When I was in college I promptly lost my faith, and I was looking at all types of spirituality. But despite the fact that I became a secularist, I knew there was a deeper meaning to life. Then, in my early adulthood, I noticed that I got along best with people who had grown up in a religion, even if they had left it. I developed a notion that people who grew up with a faith of some kind had an internal security that others—who had no religion or spirituality—didn't have." Embracing this observation, Dr. Hilfiker and his wife began to look for a religion they could honestly and sincerely practice after they had children. David clarifies: "I wasn't just trying to become a good parent. I believed that religion would give me something I couldn't get from anything else. So in other words, it wasn't just about what I wanted to give my kids; it was about finding out what was real."

In order for children to be grounded in a religious attitude, they have to experience their parents as being sincerely moved by their own spiritual engagement. Karin Hilfiker, the daughter of David and Marja, recently said the following about her parents' decision to move into a Christian community when she was a child: "As I am thinking ahead to having kids myself, I am intimidated by the limitations raising a child could place on my life. I take inspiration from the fact that my parents were able to do what they felt called to do, and did not limit themselves in following their hearts for the 'safety' of the family. They have lived full, rich lives and continue to do so, and I have more respect for them than if they'd lived in suburbia and done the 'proper' thing." Although Karin, now in her thirties, readily acknowledges that her two siblings may have more complaints than she has about growing up at Christ House and Joseph House, she still believes that her parents opened up invaluable spiritual opportunities through their religious commitment.

Openings

There are times in our lives, both for ourselves and our children, when a door opens wide and the "big questions" come in. Some of these times are developmental, as when we come to see how complex our universe and world are, and how small our individual identities seem by comparison. Other times are due to life changes, such as the death of a loved one or the birth of a child. And some are tiny openings—such as taking a moment to view a spiderweb with a child and being shocked at the intricate world that's contained there.

My current Buddhist teacher, Shinzen Young, is a dynamic and passionate teacher of Vipassana—a Sanskrit word that translates roughly as "seeing things as they really are" or "insight."[4] Shinzen is not an authority figure, but more like a guide on the path who confidently says, "Turn left here," or "Check the map again." Better than anyone else I know, Shinzen summarizes what it takes to open our eyes to the wisdom and unity that are immediately before us in our everyday lives.

He talks about what it must have been like for our ancestors of a thousand or so years ago, especially the people native to the Americas who lived in the woods and on the plains. He reminds us, "You can hardly stand the temperatures in the North Dakota winter now, with all of the best gear to fight the cold. Can you imagine what it was like to spend the winter there in animal skins and flimsy shelters?" For thousands of years, human beings lived in conditions that were starkly challenging. Their lives were threatened by weather, hunger, illness, and predators on a daily basis. Suffering and pain were constantly lurking. At the same time, they had few belongings and much less to be distracted by in their routines. They rose with the sun and went to sleep when the sun descended below the horizon. The simplicity of their lives made it easier for them to practice generosity, discipline, patience, diligence, and concentration. Without these they couldn't survive.

Their daily lives were filled with spiritual meaning. Every day they accomplished great tasks: helping the sun, the weather, the animals, and the earth to function. Adversity and simplicity guaranteed they'd be connected to perplexity, reverence, and wisdom. Our ancestors didn't need special practices of meditation and concentration because it was necessary to use these skills to survive.

In our comfortable, information-saturated lives, we have to go away to special places, like meditation retreats or churches and synagogues, to encounter these conditions of simplicity and adversity. Meditation retreats are usually demanding, quiet, and full of mystery. The silence, the physical and mental exertion of sitting still for hours, the crowded spaces, the sharing of food and sleeping quarters, and the focus on concentration and equanimity guarantee that each and every participant will encounter a new spiritual discovery—large or small, something of her or his own inherent wisdom.

If you can't or don't participate in such prearranged spiritual environments, everyday life still provides occasions when our awareness naturally expands and we tap into a sense of oneness or transcendence. Young children do this fairly readily, especially in circumstances where they feel relaxed or inspired: in the presence of loved ones, at the edge of a flower garden, on the beach at the ocean. I recall once when my youngest child looked at a sunflower and said, quite casually, "God is in there." He was about four years old. Since we were not in the habit of saying "God," we asked him more about it. He said that the flower was connected to the sky and that the sun put the sky into the flower. God was in the sky, and so naturally God was in the flower. He saw all of this in a flash. A child's view often has a natural simplicity and openness to mystery.

In chapter five I mentioned that the lifetime rate of depression in America has increased at least tenfold from what it was in the generation born before 1915. It's possible that the adversity and simplicity of American life were just enough greater then that contact with a sense of mystery about life was more accessible. Forced by life's difficulties to find greater internal balance, the earlier generation may have had more access to their inherent wisdom.

Obviously I am not advocating difficult living conditions, but I am suggesting that adversity, simplicity, and mystery are themes that are important for reverence and may have antidepressive effects. Roughing it on a camping trip or a hike, or simply being absolutely quiet while waiting in a long line or traffic jam, and asking your child (and yourself as well) to see what happens in his mind—these are everyday opportunities to sharpen an attunement to natural wisdom, something often just below the surface in young children. But perhaps the most available access to reverence and mystery for people of all ages is through illness and death.

Cultivating Reverence for Life and Death

Spiritual questioning and yearning arise naturally in the face of loss, illness, decline, and death. American children have been more protected from the reality of these aspects of existence than children in any other society, as far as I know. Most adults that I see in psychotherapy now have never witnessed someone die; I know because I ask. This is a terrible waste of opportunity for spiritual development. If you have never seen another person die, your own death will seem as alien as walking on another planet. If you have been with a dying person, especially through the stages of gradual dying, you will gain knowledge, confidence, and perhaps even wisdom about your own death.

American children and teens, as many educators have pointed out in their interviews with me, have grown up seeing hours upon hours of video, TV, and movie deaths and killings. These sanitized or dramatized deaths may give young people the idea that they know something about death and dying, but they don't—not until they have learned about it from someone who is dying, being in the presence of a flesh-and-blood person. "Virtual death" gives us an ersatz experience: we believe we know, but we don't. Being with a dying or dead person naturally taps into a deep religious longing, as it always has for human beings throughout time.

In other societies (and ours in the past), it is expected that children witness illness, dying, and death before they have reached adulthood. Elders and others die at home, in the living area, and sometimes their bodies are kept in view for a long period of time. My daughter was a Peace Corps volunteer in Thailand in a remote jungle village. She knew a family that kept the body of Grandmother in their living room for a year after she died! They had drained her bodily fluids and prepared her so that she wouldn't stink. She was kept in a simple wooden box in order for all members of the family to see her once more before she was cremated. Some traveled a long distance to pay their respects. Everyone in the family and all the villagers accepted a dead grandmother in the living room as a normal, everyday event. Children played right next to her coffin, and other family members ate and drank by her, often recollecting their memories of times with her.

Seeing Grandmother in this condition opens us, and especially children, to questions about the meaning of a human life.

Here's what Karin Hilfiker says about having seen illness and death in her teen years: "Too many kids get sheltered from the reality of death. It was very powerful for me to see, be around, and experience it, and to carry it with me, even now. I check myself when I get too caught up in something—school or work or whatever. Hey, death will happen. Keep that in mind. Whether it's tomorrow or in fifty years. Will you be happy with the sum of your life? Can you cherish this moment?"

Witnessing illness and death also stirs our generosity and compassion if we allow ourselves the necessary time and attention. Like other animals, we are curious about death. When parents ask me how they can encourage their young or adolescent children to develop spiritual awareness, I always recommend having them visit the ill and dying. If a child is under the age of four or so, it is difficult for the child to understand the facts. After that age it is generally quite clear to a child what death and illness are. At any given moment in our lives, there is usually someone in our neighborhood or family who is ill or dying. And at certain moments a significant person will be on her deathbed. That's a very important time to go and be with this person—and to take your children with you. Many existential and religious questions and concerns emerge when a loved one is seriously ill or dying. It can also be useful to visit those whom you don't know well, because you may discover a surprisingly fundamental connection with them that transcends the personal. Mother Teresa often talked about how grateful she had been to be at the side of strangers who were dying, to be with them in such an intimate way. Since we will all decline (or have an accident) and die, we have a universal connection through death.

When Karin thinks back to her teenage years, she sees her encounters with AIDS and death as a "perfect antidote to all the bullshit of high school pettiness, clothes, college applications, parties, drinking, sex, and gossip. Having something that was profound and spiritual—without preaching or dogma—was a perfect outlet. Those other things were silly. This was *real*." The word "real" comes up again. The closer that we come to the real world—where we know absolutely that we are limited, vulnerable, dependent on others, and responsible for our own decisions—the better. Karin continues: "I got to cry at the funerals, which I did, copiously. I often found myself crying and crying with my mind wandering to some fight with my friend, or pressure at school, or some unnamed sorrow."

That "unnamed sorrow" may correspond to the conscious and unconscious losses that she had suffered in her own life. Recognizing and talking about our losses is a way to increase our reverence for life. Dr. David Landers, the psychology professor at Saint Michael's College whom I interviewed, mentioned that most college students have known friends who have died in high school. "Almost every kid I know has had a friend who died in high school from an alcohol or drug or accident event. How is that dealt with in families? I know when my niece lost a friend who was driving the car, and another kid riding in the car, through an accident, she said she wanted to go to the wake. My sister asked her, 'Would you like me to go with you?' and my niece said, 'No, I'm going with a group of my friends.' And they did. I don't know if she talked with her friends or if she talked with her family afterward, but I think it's an important thing to talk about when it happens."

It is important to talk about death with your family and friends: about what you and others believe happens after we die. Everyone has an idea about it, and many people have had deep insights but few opportunities to discuss them with others. Children, especially, often have profound insights about death, because they don't yet have the cultural baggage of self-consciousness and skepticism.

When you talk to your kids or your friends about death,

don't assume that it should have a simple story, like falling asleep or being the last frame of a movie. Even if you have been persuaded that death means a "flat line on the EEG" or "nothing," remain open to your own and others' intuitions and insights. Ask open-ended questions, such as "What happens after we die?" If you draw a blank when you think about your own ideas of death, then stay with the blank and see what feelings or images arise. Be assured that death has meaning for everyone. Dr. Robert Thurman, a professor of Buddhist studies at Columbia University, reminds us in the introduction to his translation of *The Tibetan Book of the Dead* to be curious, even suspicious, about our materialistic equation of death with sleep or nothingness.

> *When we see this equation, we can understand at once why materialists scoff at spiritual or religious forms of liberation. Why would they need it? They have already guaranteed themselves permanent rest. They have a guaranteed nothingness waiting for them, attained without the slightest effort on their part, without ethical sacrifice, without realization, without developing any skill or knowledge. All they have to do is fall asleep, a skill they have already cultivated during thousands of nights.*[5]

When teens and children are allowed to speak openly about what they think happens after death, they will almost universally express some version of an afterlife or at least some questions about it.[6]

Dr. Landers ran a grief support group at Saint Michael's for a year and a half. "We met every week, and we had students and faculty and staff. And all the students had lost someone. And then a woman joined our group who was dying of cancer. It was fascinating for everyone. This woman could help the students understand what it was like to have cancer and be dying, and the students could talk about what it was like when their family member had died. It was unbelievable. So powerful. Probably some of the most powerful work I've done at the college. It was amazing to bring different generations together and talk about death and see it happening at the same time."

Every eighteen minutes someone commits suicide in the United States, and suicide is the third leading cause of death for people aged fifteen to twenty-four, according to psychologist Jean Twenge.[7] Many parents know someone who has had a child who committed suicide. Every parent would do anything to provide a safeguard against a child's committing suicide, but most rarely consider that developing a reverence for life, through a knowledge of death, could provide such a protective factor.

When I encounter suicidal ideas, desires, or plans in a client in psychotherapy, I always ask, "What are you wanting to accomplish by killing yourself?" Inevitably I get the answer that Robert Thurman describes as the "materialist equation" of sleep and death. People want to commit suicide to end their suffering—no surprise. But when we sit with the dying, we begin to see that death is not a simple ending. First, we learn that many or most of the dying encounter a life review—some kind of review of how they have affected others and what they have contributed in terms of kindness and care. The movement from life into death brings an accounting for the life they've just had. What's more, many dying people report that they are joined in the process by loved ones who are already dead. Nothing interferes more with a suicidal wish than seriously considering that it may be just that—a wish—and that suffering may continue after death, complicated by suicide.

The natural limitations of life transform the demands of the self-esteem trap. Obsessive self-focus, restless dissatisfaction, and impossible desires for success or control just drop away in the presence of serious illness, dying, and death (our own or someone else's). A reverence for life—which often comes quickly in the face of death—can diminish the grip of feeling special or defective in one fell swoop. A person not only feels gratitude and compassion for human life, but also fears losing it and the wisdom it can bring.

What's Vital

It doesn't matter if your children end up agreeing with you about the details of your religious beliefs, but it matters a great deal that they see you sincerely pondering the mystery of life with a childlike wonder and earnestness to find out what's real. It matters that children see their parents developing a religious attitude and practicing good character. If you are an adult for whom this hasn't been the case, then you have to take your own steps to deepen your genuine spiritual search for a practice that can help you understand what it means to love, to be of service, to know the truth, and to sustain hope amid the suffering and misery of life. And as odd as it may sound, even from a young age, look into the adventure of death. Keeping death on your shoulder deepens your engagement with life, moment to moment.

With young children it's easy to talk openly about what to notice and what's mysterious in daily life. They readily see it. Talk about awe and mystery, saying, for instance, how strange it is that we find ourselves here in a galaxy where ours is the only inhabited planet we know in a vast universe that is far denser and more complex than it looks to our naked eyes. Make sure that you let your young ones know how you ponder the bigger questions of your existence. Tell them about your perplexity and about the insights you've had and about the vastness of what's out there. Take extra time in your trips back and forth to town or school to look at things that are changing with the seasons. And if something new emerges, pay close attention. For instance, this summer we've been watching a robin build her nest, warm her eggs, and raise her young, with the help of her partner, right outside the window that's midway up the stairs to our second floor. It's impossible to go past our clear view of the nest without stopping to see what's happening. Even teenagers appreciate a drama like this.

Don't underestimate the important role a religious attitude plays in bringing greater calm and meaning to family life. But don't *pretend* to have one, because it will only undermine your children's openness to the spiritual possibilities that life offers. Instead find an approach that truly brings you in touch with reverence, awe, and mystery, and share that with your kids. Even simple rituals—such as lighting some candles and pausing to watch them—can bring into view some of your own inherent wisdom and will certainly do the same for your children.

Recently I came across an article in the *New York Times* about a program in mindfulness in several public schools throughout the country: "In the Classroom, a New Focus on Quieting the Mind."[8] This program is teaching kids how to "lead a balanced life" by calling them to attention, striking a bowl-chime bell, and asking them to close their eyes and take a moment just to breathe. Although some teachers were dubious about how this could be helpful, the principal said, "If we can help children slow down and think, they have the answers within themselves." (It's true for teenagers and adults too, but just a little harder for us to believe it.) One of the third graders said that mindfulness made her feel "calm, like something on *Oprah*."

Her classmate said that "it feels like when a bird cracks open its shell."

For some of us the blending of a religious attitude with good character will include, or even demand, practicing simplicity and concentration in a meditative environment. Others will find religion and character moving them more readily to helping others, practicing kindness and service. Overall, though, it's best if you can develop both—in interaction with your family members—in a way that's most interesting to you and/or your children. One simple way to begin is to follow the six practices that I described in chapter six. A sincere religious attitude should strengthen empathy and compassion for self and others while being spiritually refreshing, as when a bird cracks open its shell.

Discovering a spiritual dialogue between your own meditative insights and serving others—and helping your kids do the same—sharpens your awareness of interdependence, the most profound truth about our existence. Deepening our love for others while expanding our connection to a spiritual source is a natural antidote to the demands of a special self and any pressure to feel superior to others. In the next chapter I examine the unique emotional landscape of human love, which can often seem overwhelming, especially if it's not grounded in a religious attitude or a spiritual practice.

CHAPTER EIGHT

Love and Its Near Enemy

Love provides its own lessons in adversity, requires a good conscience, grows from our compassion, and demands autonomy in order to flourish. Love also depends on commitment and discipline, but many of us take it for granted, feeling almost casual about it. If stopped on the street and asked "Is love in your life?" we'd probably answer in the affirmative and give it little thought. On any ordinary day, people claim to love the weather, their cars, their pets, their children, and their life partners (not necessarily in that order). This superficial ease with love disappears when we look deeply into our lives and our feelings. On countless occasions in individual and couples psychotherapy with me, people exclaim in a serious or thoughtful moment, "I don't know if love really exists!"

True love does exist, although probably not in the form that most of us would identify as love. Love connects us and pulls us apart. It builds our marriages, our families, and our hopes and dreams, but it also destroys them. Human love is more like rocks grinding up against each other—smoothing out the rough edges or shattering each other—than like streams flowing together. Love is hard and tiring, filled with heartache and longing as much as it is filled with joy and wonder. Only a few of us know how to love well, but if we don't know how to love, we don't know how to live well.

Most of us think of love in terms of the comfort, passion, closeness, or beauty it will bring us. We imagine the enjoyment of passing hours and days with our beloved, who pleases us in touch, smell, and conversation. Perhaps we even think of living happily ever after. Unfortunately this is not love but its intoxicating sibling, idealization. Buddhists use the term "near enemy" to mean a superficial or misleading twin of a valuable state or attitude. In Buddhist parlance, then, we could say that idealization is the near enemy of love. If we mistake idealization for love, we can be harmfully misled in our connections to others and ourselves.

The special self is the creation of idealization. Exceptional, extraordinary, perfect: these are not the descriptions of any real human being, a person with weaknesses as well as strengths. If we have heard repeatedly how talented, beautiful, smart, or promising we are, we may grow up with an intolerance for weakness and difficulty in others, and a greater intolerance for imperfections in ourselves. Within such a self-esteem trap, we are unable to connect with others or embrace ourselves in the messy, difficult ambivalence of love.

In order to commit ourselves to love, we have to let go of our ideals for perfection and near-perfection. Instead we have to adjust to repeated disappointments, frustrations, failures, and demands (our own and others'). Above all, love requires us to be realistic in our expectations, tolerant of limitations, and empathic with human suffering. Describing love, the psychoanalyst

Otto Kernberg quotes the poet Octavio Paz: "Love is the point of intersection between desire and reality. Love . . . reveals reality to desire."[1]

Growing up exposes all of us to the twists and turns of love. We begin in a family, a hotbed of conflicting needs, desires, and personalities. We learn our first lessons about love there. As we mature we apply these lessons again and again to our friends, our partners, our children, and our mentors. The mistakes of our past are reproduced in our present and future. Not surprisingly, how we were originally loved or idealized or needed leaves a powerful imprint on how we love others. Too many I'm Okay–You're Okay parents have innocently made the mistake of idealizing their children instead of truly loving them.

The Parent-Child Attachment Bond

To a great extent the allure of having children is the promise of being idealized and idealizing. Most of us hope to have a child whom we can adore and who looks up to us. Some people even imagine specifically that their children will be new and improved versions of themselves: shiny new mirror images. When we feel that biological clock ticking, we are not envisioning long nights waiting up for a teenager who sasses us when we ask where he's been. We're not even imagining a baby with colic who is impossible to soothe. We are thinking of cuddly pleasures and wonderful friendly encounters.

Whether or not you buy my idea that idealization is a strong pull in our reproductive desire, if you want that baby, it's probably all you can think about. It feels as though a baby will bring you all sorts of things you don't already have. At the very least your baby will bring a new attachment bond.

We form attachment bonds in order to survive. For humans

the group (family or tribe), not the individual, is the unit of survival. Attachment is the experience of identifying with another—feeling that your survival depends on the welfare of the other. That dependence is a fact for the human infant and child. This kind of identification happens in every parent-child bond, and the feelings go both ways. Children feel their acute dependence on the parent, and the parent feels an identification with the child. If something goes wrong with the child, it goes wrong for the parent as well.[2]

Attachment motivates us to keep close tabs on our bonded others. We want to know they are nearby, because our survival depends on them. The caregiver also remains very alert to the whereabouts of a young one. Humans are hardwired with something called separation anxiety, which we share with many other animals.[3] Separation anxiety gives us a shock when we notice that our bonded other has disappeared or is threatening to disappear.

Protest or rage is the first level of separation anxiety; you've witnessed this in a toddler who screams when a parent drops him off at day care. The screaming means something like, "Hey, don't leave me here; I need you and you shouldn't forget about me!" The parent feels anxious and guilty too. Following a round of such protest is a lowered mood, a kind of sadness or even depression. It expresses something like, "I've been left and now I'm done for." When life goes on, though, the toddler begins to look up and play and engage with others, maybe with a bit of vague sadness that eventually passes. There is an apparent reestablishment of status quo. But if the toddler is left for too long—if Mom doesn't come back for days—that child will seem indifferent to her when she reappears. This is called apathy. You see it in children who are separated from their parents for long periods or are orphaned. Apathy seems to be a biological response that prevents our spending too much energy in protest or despair. Life must go on. If a child is actually abandoned by parents, life goes forward in only a very fragile way, as the pain of grief sinks in.

Grief, as we all know, is a form of depression that occurs when we lose someone with whom we are bonded.[4] Our hearts are broken, and they are never entirely healed, although we can move forward with our lives and even transform the experience into wisdom and insight. After telling our story repeatedly, we may accept our loss if we're adults; but for children grief can be simply a terrible physical and emotional pain.

Once you've formed an attachment bond, you have identified yourself with that other. You are then vulnerable to separation anxiety if there's a threat to your bond, and to grief if it's broken. Even if you lose your affection for the other person, you will still feel anxiety and grief if your bond is broken. An attachment bond is not the same thing as love. As we shall see, we can in fact form attachment bonds with people (say, sexual partners) whom we don't even like. It's important to understand the power of attachment, but also not to confuse it with love.

A knowledge of how attachment is different from love helps us understand separations from those to whom we are attached (parents, partners, or children). If your parent or child leaves without warning or is suddenly missing, you'll feel the emotions of separation anxiety (protest, despair, apathy). You can anticipate that you will "punish" that person (consciously or unconsciously) when he returns. Separation anxiety motivates us to lash out at those attached others who leave us; our welfare is entangled with theirs. This makes sense of the fact that parents may lash out at a child who's been missing when that child comes back.

The long dependency of a human childhood requires that we

rely a great deal on our attachment bonds to keep us close to those who sustain us. When children are growing up, they are learning how to love over their entire childhood. Until they know how to love, they will idealize, identify with, and be bonded with their parents. This is not love.

To truly love another, we must know who the other is — seeing and accepting our differences in motivations, abilities, style, personality, and so on. Children only gradually develop this kind of knowing as they form a superego that allows them to see how they are the same as and different from others. Until children can really know and appreciate another as a separate being, they depend on attachment bonds and idealization to keep them close to those they need.

Even in relation to peers and siblings, young children basically have two ways of recognizing another: like me or not like me. By the end of adolescence, if all has gone well, children are able to appreciate others as distinct beings with differences that are truly interesting. As parents we have an option that a growing child does not have: we can truly love our children and not simply idealize, admire, or bond with them.

Idealizing Our Children

To truly love our children, who are not yet able to see and know us personally, is a great achievement. We assume that parents can do it, although our society gives them few or no tools for understanding the contradictions that are inherent in loving. In place of a knowledge about human love, parents are fed fictions of parental love that confuse it with idealization and attachment. In the fictions, good (maybe even great) parents are portrayed as giving their children endless attention, affection, and resources — everything the children want — and in return the parents are rewarded one day by having produced grown-up individuals who are self-confident, empathic, loving, able to achieve whatever goals they set for themselves, and happy to care for their aging parents. These fictional adult children reflect the merits of the good parenting they received. After all that parental sacrifice, according to the fictions, the children will be grateful and generous. I'm Okay–You're Okay parents idealize not only their children, but parental love itself.

Of course it's perfectly normal to idealize an infant. Parents almost have to idealize a new baby, because infants are so demanding of time, energy, and services that if we viewed them realistically, the human race would come to a crashing halt. But in order for children and parents to develop functional healthy relationships (in which parents are the leaders, helping their children become members of a family and society), the idealization of a baby should begin to shift after about the first six months at the latest.[5] If instead idealization replaces love over time, a parent will become enmeshed or identified with the child.

Idealization is a pressure or demand on the beloved to be the perfect other: a mirror image of ourselves or the image of what would complete us. If idealization continues too long, the special self of the child becomes the special resource of the parent. The parent has to protect the image of the child at all costs. When a parent *always* prefaces any word of complaint with a compliment (for instance, "Sam is such a bright boy, that's why he doesn't pay attention to his teacher, he's just bored"), I can tell that the child is being used as a resource for the parent's self-esteem. You should be able to complain straightforwardly about your kid, because your kid causes you a lot of trouble in addition to bringing you joy.

Sometimes idealization becomes a norm and a parent stops expressing any negative feelings about a child and may even stop feeling any. But children know that they are both good and bad. They are thrown off balance when an adult seems to feel otherwise, although they perceive the power advantage and may not want to give it up. Children like Erin or Adrienne will feel a pressure, perhaps only a subtle one, to protect their "golden" status, but later on they'll be caught in the self-esteem trap, with its pursuit of illusory ideals and resources.

In order for families to have golden children, they also have to have scapegoats—other siblings, a parent, a stepmother, a stepfather. Someone has to be hated, devalued, or denigrated in order for someone else to be elevated. The negative feelings that would have been expressed to the golden child are siphoned off to another in the family or close to the family.[6]

Deprived of the taste of reality, a golden child may be confused or shocked when she goes out into the world. Golden children know very well how to be desirable, and they expect to feel the warm glow of others' praise, admiration, attention, and affection. When this isn't forthcoming, the golden child falls into the confusion and anxiety of the self-esteem trap. Although he may not behave openly like he has a special self, that pressure to be perfect is always under the surface.

America's newly identified at-risk group for high levels of emotional disorders (especially anxiety and depression), as Madeleine Levine reports in her 2006 book, *The Price of Privilege*, are preteens and teens from affluent families, meaning those earning $120,000 per year and more. Their vulnerability goes against our stereotypes. These are not families where children are neglected, but rather where parents are overinvolved. Many of these helicopter or role-reversal parents have an idealized enmeshment with their children, unknowingly wanting a child to complete the parent's fantasy of perfection or fame. Current studies suggest that 30 to 40 percent of twelve-to-eighteen-year-olds from affluent homes are experiencing disturbing psychological symptoms.[7] These statistics reflect the confusion between love and idealization among many I'm Okay–You're Okay parents. Not only do these parents provide too many material things and privileges, fail to keep their children accountable, and over-praise, but they hold up a distorting mirror. It reflects, "You're perfect because you're mine."

Parental idealization can make teens and young adults almost addicted to talking with their parents. Cell phones allow college students to be in touch with their helicopter parents several times a day. Dr. David Landers, from Saint Michael's College, says that parent-child enmeshment was one of the biggest problems he faced when he was director of the college counseling center. Dr. Landers finds that parents are using their children to feel better about themselves. "I had a mother call me to tell me that her daughter calls her every day at 10 AM to complain about the college; she calls and spends about a half hour on the phone. The mother wanted to know what to do, and I told her, 'Don't answer the phone.' She said, 'But she's so distraught, and she doesn't have anyone to talk to.' I said, 'Trust me, she'll find someone else. Maybe you need to find someone else to talk to yourself.' "

Landers believes that a lack of realism—there's that word "real" again—is the problem of these helicopter parents who hover around their children. Many helicopter parents "are so enmeshed in their children's lives that they don't have their own lives. If I could give one piece of advice to today's parents it would be, 'Get a life for yourself. Go to a movie, read a book, get out of the house so that you're not always available on that telephone. It's okay to be a friend to your child, but don't try to be your child's best friend.' I see too many mothers who want to be their kids' best friends, and they want to be friends with their children's friends. This is weird. Children aren't supposed to be with their parents all of their life!" Idealizing a child or a parent instead of loving that person replaces a healthy relationship with distortion and enmeshment. When young people who are caught in such an enmeshment step out on their own to find a relationship with a partner, they may get caught in the self-esteem trap because they can't find that mirror that reflects, "You're perfect because you're mine."

Cultivating ordinariness in our children and ourselves, showing and teaching them how to share and collaborate with others, vastly improves their chances of letting go of unrealistic desires and loving their partners in adulthood. In the example we set and the preparation we give our children, we must emphasize the need for modesty, tolerance, and self-correction in steering the course of love. The parent-child bond, the life partner bond, the sibling bond, and the friendship bond all depend on our being able to reflect realistically on ourselves, especially on our faults and limitations. As our children grow in their autonomy and prepare themselves for love in their adult lives, they need to learn how to make good use of criticism, and how to check themselves to see what is really going on. They need to learn the nature of true love.

The Flux of Love

All life experience can be seen as an expression of a constant flux of expansion and contraction. Our moment-to-moment breath, our hopes and dreams, world events, our health, and the weather are just a few ways we can readily notice the fluctuation of expanding and contracting. Some moments in life are open and promising, while others are closed and negating. In order to accept ourselves, our lives, and those we want to love, we have to embrace both expansion and contraction. This is especially hard when it comes to love.

Most people define love as an expansive feeling. They want it to be warm, inviting, and welcoming. They want to feel an identification with the beloved. But true love is ambivalent —sometimes expansive and sometimes contractive—because it includes a tolerance and acceptance of the other person's limitations and a commitment to the other person's freedom to be the person he or she is. In every loving relationship, we are expected to feel and accept the contractive aspects of anxiety, hate, disappointment, tolerance, loyalty, responsibility, fear for the future, and a visceral sense that the beloved is "other" (our opposite, enemy, interrogator, or evil twin). The expansive feelings of comfort, pleasure, affection, trust, joy, wonder, and a visceral sense that the beloved is "self" (just like me) are far more welcome than the contractive ones.

Growing up in a family guarantees exposure to both the expansive and the contractive aspects of love. Conflicts of needs between parents, between parents and children, and among siblings provide an arena in which we learn to tolerate a mix of ups and downs in ongoing affectionate relationships. Yet if a child is only idealized by a parent, those invaluable first lessons about a human relationship are distorted. In place of the natural development of disillusionment in the parent-child relationship, idealization preserves a childish fantasy of a perfect child or a perfect parent.

Disillusionment is the effect of our hopes and illusions being dashed, like rocks that shatter when they crash down a cliff. Our illusions break apart and we feel negative emotions—anger, anxiety, shame, guilt, sadness—that darken our image of the beloved. What we had so desired, or hoped for, even for the good of our beloved, is not happening, is not real. Love reveals reality to desire. This kind of disillusionment brings into view our commitment to the beloved.

Our first responsibility as parents is to teach our children basic human values—to cherish life, to speak the truth, to respect the things of others, to use sexuality in a caring and responsible way. Our second responsibility is to disentangle ourselves from our own idealizing enmeshment. The world of the future is not the world of the past. Our child will not be like us, because she is a person of her own times. As parents, we must commit to preparing our beloved child to become an autonomous, loving adult—an ordinary human being. Unless we commit ourselves to helping her develop these skills, she is likely to be at risk for a restless dissatisfaction that may manifest itself as depression, anxiety, or addiction.

A most significant contractive aspect of parental love is a willingness to discipline our children. My parents, like most of my friends' parents, were strict. They had rules, regulations, and punishments. I never doubted that my parents cared about me, but I knew that I had to obey their rules or I would be punished. When my mother would sit down and give me a ceremonious spanking ("You know what this is for, and you will learn not to do that again"), she always added, "This is hurting me more than it's hurting you." I didn't believe her at the time, but once I became a parent I knew exactly what she meant. Holding our children to standards of good behavior and moral conduct means being willing to use our negative emotions to express discipline and punishment. This is a part of our love for them.

When I disciplined my children by withholding privileges, giving lectures, and making them sit still or sometimes even stand in a corner (yes, it's true), I would think back to my mother's saying that punishing me hurt her. By the time my children were nine or ten years old, they would sometimes say "I hate you!" when I lectured them or criticized their behavior. Although I would not have been allowed to say that to my mother, I actually felt their words were an honest expression of their authentic, understandable feelings. And I would respond, "Of course you hate me. I'm your mother." Who else could be more hateable? I was the most important person in their young lives, and my critical responses were painful for them. I assumed that their hate was strong because their connection to me was also strong, even though I hated hearing they hated me. It is natural for parents, too, to feel a mix of hate and love in their relationships with their children.

As parents we shouldn't be ashamed of our ambivalent feelings toward our children, but rather use them to sharpen our wisdom and our objectivity. Ambivalence provides both children and parents the opportunity to learn frustration tolerance and to find equanimity with negative feelings and thoughts (without necessarily expressing them), as a means of building good character.[8] And good character is a lifelong protection against the self-esteem trap. By the time a child arrives at late adolescence, she should know that true love is ambivalent and requires the toleration of hateful feelings. She should understand that love demands a commitment to the welfare of the other and is not based primarily on pleasant feelings and pleasing others. True love means that we keep the beloved's freedom and welfare in our hearts, no matter how we feel at any given moment. Obviously, good parents can learn to love their children in this way, but grown-up children should be expected to learn to love their parents this way as well.

True Love

In a culture like ours, which confuses love with idealization, loving our children is, as I said before, a truly great achievement. All along we must make use of the six practices of being ordinary that I described in chapter six: generosity, discipline, patience, diligence, concentration, and wisdom. These will help us to hold lightly the expansive joys and dreams and the contractive hatreds and disillusionments. In this comprehensive embrace, we will provide an invaluable resource for our growing child and practice the highest form of human engagement.

True love is the willingness always to return with interest, warmth, and compassion to a person whom you know well and see clearly, no matter how disillusioned you become. It is a willingness to speak honestly but kindly of the other's faults and failures (in addition to talents and strengths), and with children, to guide them toward truth and virtue, no matter how uncomfortable their responses make you feel. It is the knowledge that you will be loyal, but not foolish, in standing up for their goodness if it's challenged, doing what you can to enlarge their welfare.

Love means that you take a distant view of yourself, not only in regard to seeing yourself as utterly human and nothing special, but also in knowing your own range of habits, limitations, and madness so that you can be responsible for them. You don't want to inflict your weaknesses or your demons on your beloved any more than you absolutely have to. In the midst of all this, you also have to be willing to feel your contractive feelings without blaming the other person for them. Having patience with your negative feelings lets you discover why you feel them so intensely: because you care so much about the other's welfare.

When a child is loved this way by a parent or another elder, that child has the possibility of loving herself in the same way—even in adolescence, but certainly in adulthood. If that child can love herself as an ordinary human being with certain strengths and lots of limitations, that grown-up child will be free to love others and will not feel trapped in an endless drive to replenish depleted self-esteem. One published example of this kind of love has stayed with me over the years. It's from a 1993 book by writer Nancy Mairs, *Ordinary Time*.[9]

In her account of her love for her teenage son, Matthew — born jaundiced, Rh-incompatible with her, and separated from her for his first week in an isolette — she first describes the contractive aspects of her feelings about him. His birth, she says, is the "one great tragedy" of her life. Her initial separation from Matthew, she believes, propelled him into a restless and insecure attachment to her. "From the outset he cried through most of his waking hours, all the more fiercely if I held and cuddled him; grief-stricken at his rejection, I retreated into the role of caretaker, dutiful enough but distant and wary. For years, I believed that I didn't love him." [10]

As he entered his teens, she could barely stand the sight of him: "Both sides of his head shaved, the hair on top sticking up in clumps. Neck and arms draped with chains and padlocks, studded strips of leather, filthy camouflage bandannas, loud neckties." She refused to idealize him the way that his father and grandparents did. They subscribed to the theory that "inside this hideous exterior is a heart of gold, a fine upstanding young man, a brilliant student, impeccably dressed and aesthetically refined, if one could find the key to set him free. I don't subscribe. There's only one Matthew. What you see is what you get. So let him be." [11]

She goes on to say that gradually she realized that her complicated feelings — grief at his rejection, terror for his well-being, guilt for endangering him, interest and attention to the minute details of his life, defense of his freedom to choose for himself — are the marks of love. With this, she awakened: "Everything in my experience and education had suggested that 'love' was reactive, an upwelling of delight caused by the beloved's pleasing looks or ways. My beloved did not please me. In fact, much of the time he drove me stark ravers. But he absorbed me utterly. And still does." [12]

She talks about "playing computers" with Matthew, noting his grace and the swiftness of his mind, his tact in teaching her. He reassures her, she being disabled with multiple sclerosis, that they are having fun. And she knew it was true. In her love of Matthew, Nancy Mairs sees the love of God:

> *If this is love—and it is—then I can faintly glimpse what the love of God might be. So long as I understood it as a response to my pleasingness—if I was good, then God would love me (and contrariwise, if I was bad, then God would throw me into hell, the most hateful gesture imaginable)—I couldn't believe in it, since the chances of my ever being good enough to merit the love of God were slenderer than a strand of silk. But suppose God takes no particular delight in me at all. Suppose God finds me about as attractive as I found Matthew during the years when razor blades dangled from his ears and his room was littered with plates and glasses growing long green hairs and his favorite band was called Useless Pieces of Shit. Suppose God keeps me steadily in sight, agonizing over my drunken motorcycle rides, failed courses, laughing at my jokes, putting in earplugs at my gigs, signing for my release at the police station, weeping with me as we bury the dead dog. . . . Oh, I feel certain that she does.* [13]

And I feel certain too.

Our willingness to return again and again to the beloved no matter what he has done, and to commit ourselves to knowing that person, while allowing both the expansive and contractive sides of love, is a human miracle. No other animal can do it, because no other animal feels the range and complexity of responses that we feel toward the beloved and ourselves. When we know that we can work with ourselves and with the beloved no matter what, then we have the stable foundation of an eternal love.

The Myth of Romance

Just as there is a dangerous mistaken fiction of an idealized parental love, there is a similar fiction of an idealized romantic love that drives our teenage and young adult children. Indeed America is a romance-hungry culture. Romance is a drug. It pumps you up with fantasies and dreams — about the beloved and yourself. Our children, like us, have seen so many romantic comedies and TV shows that they believe that fanciful, idealized love is possible. With all this fantasy, a mutually romantic encounter with a potential partner or lover can be a little like being thrown into a psychotic projection: idealized self meets idealized self and both people feel like gods.

GenMe teens and young adults are as romance starved as the Boomers were, but GenMe is more cynical and jaded about finding the Right Person. When you've grown up with I'm Okay–You're Okay parents, first and foremost you want to find a soul mate who values *your* personal worth. When you fail, you can back away into cynicism and you'll find plenty of support from your friends.

There is little in our media that shows the transition from romance to love. In fact when the desire-soaked HBO series *Sex and the City* tried to introduce love near the end of the run of the show, the script was flat and unconvincing. Instead of crossing the terrain from romance through disillusionment to intimacy, couples on the show broke up repeatedly because they couldn't locate anyone who might qualify for idealization. If you're looking for someone who will put you on a pedestal, or if you're looking to put someone else there, then it's romance and not love that you're after.

American young people now marry later than any previous generation, typically in their early to middle thirties. Before marriage there are usually a number of breakups of serious relationships that have lasted from two to ten years—a type of minidivorce. One result of contemporary dating styles, cohabiting, and the higher divorce rate is that more than one out of three people aged twenty-five to twenty-nine lives alone or with a roommate. In some cities adults will spend more than half their lives alone. And in the age bracket of twenty-five to thirty-nine, there are more unmarried men than unmarried women, making loneliness an equal-opportunity experience.[14] Naturally this increases anxiety, depression, and addictions. Moving from one romance to another, without the knowledge of how to transform it into love, is exhausting and emotionally draining.

If people are sexually involved during a romance, as is usually the case, they also develop an attachment bond, and then the emotions become serious. As I described earlier, an attachment bond is the experience of identifying with another—feeling that your survival depends on the connection to the other. When we take a sexual partner, we form a bond with that person. Usually after having sex several times together, a couple becomes "pairbonded." Then (just as in childhood) there's a tendency to identify with, and even want to know the whereabouts of, your pair-bonded partner. The more we have sex with someone, the more we strengthen that bond, and then we feel separation anxiety if there is a threat to the bond—even if we bring the threat on ourselves by imagining that we will break up the relationship. This is one reason people become enraged if they find out their partner has lied about being involved with someone else, even if the partner is no longer very attractive to them. Protest or rage is the first expression of separation anxiety, followed by despair or depression, and eventually apathy.

When teenage or adult pair-bonded couples are in a period of threat to their bond — before they have ended their relationship — they often feel waves of rage, despair, and apathy. In breaking an intimate attachment bond, the partners experience grief — the painful physical and/or emotional experience of loss. It's important for our teenage children to learn that you instinctively form a bond with someone with whom you have had a romance and a sexual relationship. There's no such thing as "free sex" from the perspective of our attachment instinct. Biologically, this attachment bond protects the family that might result from having sex. A pair-bonded romance isn't love, but the pain of losing it can make you wary of love, even in your teenage years. No wonder young people can become cynical.

From Romance into Love

Transforming romance into love, as I described in my 1994 book, *You're Not What I Expected: Love After the Romance Has Ended,* means going through the bleak territory of disillusionment and power struggle — becoming tolerant of the ways in which your partner disappoints you and reminds you emotionally of some of your worst experiences in growing up. We need to teach our children (as well as show them) that in matters of love you repeatedly have to take a more objective view of yourself and your habits as well as of your partner and her or his habits. You must become more flexible in your desires and reactions so that you can accept the limitations of your partner while taking responsibility for your own shortcomings. Your partner becomes a real person—separate and different from you, no longer on a pedestal, having many limitations that you had hoped to avoid.

Everything I have said about love for our children can also be applied to relationships with life partners. The one big difference between the parent-child and the life partner bond is, of course, that life partners are equals. Since they are equals, neither is in the position of being in charge of the other person. This is both easier and harder than being a parent. It's easier because you are not responsible for turning your partner into a functional, autonomous adult. It's harder because you are not responsible for turning your partner into a functional, autonomous adult. You have to accept the level of functional autonomy your partner has, just as you have to accept differences in taste, daily rhythms, values, habits, styles, and so on. If you already know what true love is and feel it in your commitment to your partner's welfare, then accepting differences comes more easily. When you repeatedly accept these differences and even find them intriguing, then your relationship can be called love. Children raised with too much praise and indulgence, and too little discipline and guidance, have a particularly hard time coping with the normal demands of ambivalence in adult love.

Loving a partner just as he or she is requires equanimity—that gentle, matter-of-fact awareness of what's actually going on. Those of us who are married or in marriagelike relationships must move from romance to disillusionment and then into a lifelong friendship in order to keep our love alive. A loving life partnership is a friendship—plus sex, the business of a household, and perhaps shared responsibility as parents. This is a complicated, many-faceted, and demanding set of involvements. It's almost too bad that it all starts with romance. We need to let our children know that every couple falls hard from that expansive, starry-eyed fantasy into the contractive reality of annoyance, frustration, competition, and negotiation that are part of everyday dealings with a life partner.

Tolerating contractive feelings is a particular challenge for GenMe'ers who are hungry for idealization and admiration, perhaps also seeking status or prestige through the resources or good looks of a partner. The normal disillusionments of romance—when faults and difficulties make a potential partner seem ugly or inferior and power struggles abound—are frightening. GenMe'ers tend to run the other way. They assume that they've chosen the wrong person. The fact is they'd have to stick around longer in order to find out. The demands of the self-esteem trap can undermine the generosity, patience, and diligence that are necessary to turn disillusionment into intimate friendship. When you make this transformation, you reap the benefits of many years of good conversations, rich conflicts, and all kinds of mutual pleasures, as well as provide a model of true love for any children that result from the union.

This kind of lifelong friendship can become a foundation for spiritual development as well, for a parent or young adult. A true spiritual friend says the same thing to your face as behind your back, watches out for your ethical and spiritual welfare, and does everything possible to help you be an ordinary and realistic human being. These principles for friendship can be applied to any long-term relationship, with a partner or a grown child. Help your friend be realistic while taking his point of view into consideration. At the heart of true friendship is a commitment to reflect mindfully on our thoughts and feelings before we act on them. In this reflective space, we feel our feelings and hear our thoughts, allowing them to be just as they are. We attempt to be truthful to ourselves about what's actually going on within us. Whatever we choose to say to our friend, we speak honestly but kindly, and allow the rest of our thoughts and feelings to fall away. The foundation for this kind of friendship is laid down through the practices of being ordinary that I described earlier.

Expectations for ourselves to be ideal or to find the ideal in our child or partner are misleading when it comes to love. In contrast to any idealized fantasy, true love has both expansive and contractive aspects. While we enjoy the expansive, we need to use the contractive wisely for our own and our children's development. If you are familiar with both sides of love—from a childhood in which you were loved rather than idealized—then you will be ready to embrace the demands of love in adulthood. This is the best promise for happiness and living well.

CHAPTER NINE

The Truth About Happiness

The truth about happiness is that we can't pursue it directly nor can we give it to others. Like self-esteem, happiness is a by-product of how we think, what we believe, and how we act. Yet there are ways of thinking, believing, and acting that make happiness more likely than not. As children or adults, we will be much happier if we embrace opportunities to learn from our mistakes and reject opportunities to think of ourselves in unrealistically positive or negative ways. Realistic self-assessment and accountability are tied to our happiness. They produce a healthy psychological immune system that protects us when we encounter the slings and arrows of fate or feel trapped in feelings of humiliation, shame, or blame. But even when we do what we can to encourage it, happiness is not guaranteed on any given day of our lives.

Unhappiness, on the other hand, *is* guaranteed. As we've seen repeatedly, discontent and adversity are part of life; there's no way to escape them. When you recognize that they are universal, then you don't always take your roadblocks and bad days personally. You don't use them to attack yourself or others. Nor do you spend large amounts of energy in vain attempts to protect your children from life's trials. You can roll with them, learn from them, tolerate your negative feelings, and begin to see your own strengths and weaknesses. This openness to life's limitations will generally make you and your children happier. We cannot escape life's difficulties, but we can change our attitude toward them.

The trouble with being special, as we've seen, is that it leads us toward pervasive unhappiness and negative self-absorption: anxiety, depression, fears of being humiliated or defective, restless dissatisfaction, pressures to be exceptional, unreadiness to take on adult responsibilities, and feelings of superiority (or inferiority). Symptoms of being special have sadly plagued those GenMe'ers and their parents who, like most of us, have been caught in the self-esteem trap of believing that everyone's a winner and can accomplish something great. The antidote to this widespread cultural attitude is not to believe that everyone's a loser with nothing to contribute. Instead we've found that an overfocus on the individual self—as an isolated, separate unit—is the mistake that we have all made in raising our children in the past three decades or so. As human beings we are fundamentally social, and we cannot consider our individual self-confidence, self-esteem, or achievement without accounting for that relatedness.

Good character and virtues support our relatedness. They allow us to feel more in touch with the reality of our actions and feelings. When we don't lie, cheat, or steal, we can be more trusting and authentic—freer in all our dealings with our families, communities, and the world. Then it's easier to be self-determining, because we don't need to keep secret anything we've done or said.

As we've taken stock of ourselves and our relationships in these pages, we have seen that there is a way to embrace success and creativity without the liabilities of being special. It's something that we've called being ordinary, and we have fleshed it out in terms of learning how best to contact our interdependence and make use of our autonomy.

Autonomy and Happiness

You might think that autonomy—making good decisions for yourself and feeling confident about your ability to direct your life—would not relate very closely to happiness. But there's research to say that it does. People find it very gratifying to exercise autonomy, not only for what it brings, but also for what it feels like. As psychologist and researcher Daniel Gilbert says in his 2006 book, *Stumbling on Happiness,* "We have a large frontal lobe so that we can look into the future, we look into the future so that we can make predictions about it, we make predictions about it so that we can control it—but why do we want to control it at all?" Even though we human beings are notoriously poor predictors about what will make us happy, he says, we enjoy the experience of wanting to do something and then doing it.[1] As I said in chapter five, starting from the beginning of our lives, we love to make things happen. Part of that pleasure is the perceived control—the sense that you are in control, whether or not you are. Clinical depression is a condition that is usually precipitated by, and always accompanied by, the loss of perceived control. Our perceived control is a wellspring of happiness when it's not associated with inner pressures and self-consciousness. In fact research suggests that if you lose your perceived control, you can become very unhappy and even possibly die from it.

In one study, researchers gave elderly residents of a local

nursing home each a houseplant. They told half the residents that they were in control of their plant's care and feeding (high-control group), and they told the remaining residents that a staff person would take responsibility for the plant's well-being (low-control group). Six months later, 30 percent of the residents in the low-control group had died, compared with only 15 percent of the residents in the high-control group. A follow-up study confirmed the importance of perceived control for the welfare of nursing-home residents.[2] Not only is this sense of control plea-surable, then, but it's also beneficial on a number of psychological and health-related levels.

Again, a family meeting is a great opportunity to hear about problem solving from each member — adults and children — as a way of illustrating autonomy: the experience of self-governance. Stories of problems and successful or failed solutions help children begin to see the meaning of learning from their own choices, whether the outcomes are wished for or not. I have stressed throughout the book that children should have the autonomy to solve their own problems and make their own choices, as appropriate to their age. Instead of thinking in terms of protecting them from negative outcomes or feelings, parents should think in terms of allowing them to experience and then express the consequences of what they tried. This is good practice for adults as well. Grappling with how we have looked at a problem and what happened, without being afraid of being wrong, is one of the most interesting, and often funniest, encounters we can have with one another. Over time people discover what helps them feel in control and happy if they can see, with the help of their friends, what to do about both positive and negative outcomes of their choices.

The fact is that we are not very good at predicting what will make us happy, nor what our future holds. For example, people work harder and harder to achieve more and earn more, even though they discover repeatedly that privilege, status, and better toys do not lead to lasting happiness. It's ironic, then, that we get such pleasure from making our own decisions and taking responsibility for our lives but are not very good at predicting what will make us happy.

Negative Experiences and Regrets

A main reason that we are bad predictors of our future is the fact that negative experiences do not affect us as painfully as we predict. When we spend a huge amount of anxiety in fretting over that low grade, the failure to get a promotion, the future effects of divorce on our children, or even a health problem, we should let ourselves know that realistically it won't matter as much as we believe. As Daniel Gilbert says, "The fact is that negative events do affect us, but they generally don't affect us as much or for as long as we expect them to." Although more than half the people in the United States will experience a trauma like rape, assault, or a natural disaster in their lifetimes, only a small fraction will develop any post-traumatic syndrome or need professional help. Resilience is the most commonly observed response to a tragic event, and not only do most people report feeling well adjusted again after a trauma, but many report a feeling of life enhancement, having learned something new from the experience.[3]

Encountering and overcoming life's adversities, as I have repeatedly said, gives us practice at regaining our balance. Gradually we build a healthy psychological immune system that, according to Gilbert, "defends the mind against unhappiness in much the same way the physical immune system defends the body against illness."[4] A healthy psychological immune system means being able to defend against some of the pain of rejection, loss, or misfortune without defending too much ("I'm clearly more accurate or knowledgeable than others, and so they're just wrong") or too poorly ("I'm a mess, and no one would love me if they saw the truth"). A healthy psychological immune system strikes a balance that will permit us some new insight from reality ("Okay, next time I'll be more polite to Aunt Minnie") without making us feel too bad. To be well defended without being defensive requires repeatedly learning from adversity. This requires practice. If children are protected from practicing by helicopter or role-reversal parents, then the children will become too defensive or defenseless when they are confronted by the difficult realities of adult life, as we've seen.

But what about regret? What should we do when facing a dilemma like the one that Erin described in graduate school or that Andrew felt in making a career choice? Many people seek psychotherapy because they fear making a big mistake in choosing poorly or believe they are the authors of their own unhappiness in having already chosen the wrong partner or career. GenMe young adults frequently come to therapy, as Andrew did, with the belief that they have to have a particular career or a certain kind of partner (making a certain amount of money and the like) in order to be happy. They have been taught to follow their dreams and not accept anything that falls short. As I said earlier, though, there is no final judgment point in life at which you find out if you went down the right path or chose the right partner. Your life unfolds from your choices, but you don't really know if you made the best ones.

Recently I saw a biographical movie about the architect Frank Gehry, whose loop-the-loop and folded buildings have been massively successful and influential in changing both the face of cityscapes and the history of American architecture.[5] In his seventies now, Gehry said that he is certain he could have just as easily become an airplane pilot. He had an interest in both aviation and architecture, but he didn't have any big opportunities to fly in his youth, whereas fate opened the door to architecture, although it wasn't easy for him to go through it. Gehry wasn't regretting choosing architecture, but noting that it was just one choice. A lot of his life has been about his choice, although he felt certain that he could have been as happy with another choice. He's probably right, according to studies of regret.

Regret is a kind of grief that we feel over some bad outcome that we believe we could have prevented. Because regret is quite painful, we want very much to avoid it. Many people have elaborate mistaken theories about regret. For example, people assume they will feel more regret if they learn about alternatives to the choices they have made, if they accept bad advice or fail to accept good advice, or if their bad choices are unconventional rather than conventional. People will use these mistaken theories in making their choices. But only one rule of thumb is a reliable guideline for avoiding regret. Studies show that people of every age and from every walk of life feel their most painful regrets about *not* doing. In other words, people feel worse about what they did not do (but wanted to do) than about what they did do that went badly—for example, not going for further education, not taking a profitable opportunity, not spending enough time with loved ones.[6] One reason people regret their inactions more than their actions is that our psychological immune system has a more difficult time being realistic about our inactions.

When we take actions that we later regret—for instance, cashing out our savings to make a trip to a Greek island during which it rains continuously—we can console ourselves with rationalizations ("After all, it was just money and I didn't have to worry about a sunburn"). But when our *inaction* leads to a lack of fulfillment, we can't console ourselves with what we learned from it. You don't learn anything from never pursuing your desires.

When an age-appropriate problem or difficulty presents itself in your child's life, encourage her to jump in and attempt to solve it. If things work out well, let her reward come directly from the situation, not mostly from your praise. If things go badly, or not as she would wish, allow her to engage with the negative feelings and outcomes, while supporting her by being confident ("I really believe that you can get through this"). Conveying directly or indirectly that she's strong enough to weather the storm helps her develop a healthier psychological immune system. Counsel your child against believing that her happiness will come mostly from external things—her appearance, grades, athletic successes—because it won't.

Those living in the shadow of the self-esteem trap find happiness to be even more elusive than the rest of us. They wrongly believe that fame, celebrity, status, or wealth should bring happiness. They're going to lose on three counts. First, it's unlikely they'll achieve their dreams for extraordinary success, because the dreams depend on rare circumstances. They'll look back on paths not taken with regret, assuming that they lost opportunities due to some fault of their own. Second, if they do get the sought-after celebrity and wealth, they'll be confused by the fact that these do not bring the rewards and satisfaction that they thought they would. And third, the demands of being special will tend to alienate them from others—from sharing, collaborating, and developing with others. Feeling like an ordinary person, instead of like someone always caught in an internal spotlight or always wanting an external one, makes it more likely that you'll feel happy when happiness actually strikes.

When Happiness Strikes

When happiness strikes, what helps us to embrace it? You might know the answer: staying in the present moment, being alert and aware. Why is it so difficult to do that, even when we're happy? Because we focus on ourselves: self-consciousness and exaggerated expectations for ourselves can interfere with even our joyful moments. If happiness is "the state of mind in which one does not desire to be in any other state," as the famous researcher of flow experience Mihaly Csikszentmihalyi says, then self-consciousness, shame, envy, jealousy, embarrassment, and guilt defeat happiness.[7] They pull us away from enjoyment into concerns about ourselves.

Envy of another will throw you off your center faster than you can blink an eye. Similarly shame and embarrassment pull you out of enjoyment and into negative feelings about yourself. All of the emotions that preoccupy us with comparisons between ourselves and others, and prompt measuring of ourselves against our expectations (Did I do that right?), explicitly limit our satisfactions.

While self-consciousness robs us of happiness, equanimity increases our happiness, whether we're children or adults. If the definition of happiness is the state of mind in which we do not desire to be in any other, then by definition equanimity enhances happiness. Equanimity, as we've seen, is that gentle, matter-of-fact awareness and acceptance of our experience, just as it is. When we have cultivated this kind of awareness, then we accept our experiences without pushing and pulling on them. No matter the feelings that are stirred, we ride the waves of expansion and contraction and remain alert. In a moment of delight, joy, or pleasure, our acceptance will increase our happiness. Doing that figure eight on ice skates, completing the pencil sketch or finishing a sculpture, or just polishing off a very good meal, we feel happy without being distracted by thinking, "Did I do that as well as I could?" "Will my work win the prize?" or "I feel stuffed! Why did I eat so much?" Indeed these kinds of self-consciousness rob us of the happiness that should be inherent in our successes and satisfactions.

Equanimity doesn't mean being passive or serene, but being able to stay in contact with the axis of your being. Equanimity gives us the freedom to return to our own wisdom. If you've just fallen down a black hole of shame and you don't close off your perceptions or start attacking yourself, but instead note your body sensations and the images that come to mind, you find that the humiliation passes quickly. You're really not thrown much off your center. Encouraging children to practice equanimity—by asking them to stop and just note their experience at random moments, such as when the phone rings or when they walk through a doorway—builds strength in their equanimity muscles that will help them over the years ahead to allow negativity to pass and to maximize pleasure.

Equanimity also supports our relationships with others. A gentle acceptance of our feelings and interactions allows us to remain empathic and connected, even when we are in conflict. We remain in contact with our humanity and open to both sides of a conflict. Especially in our close relationships, we need to retain our sense of connection through thick and thin. Most of us find this a great challenge. Envy and shame are the most disruptive feelings in close relationships. When they are activated, almost any disappointment can feel overwhelming and often leads to explosions of negative feelings and verbal attacks. As adults we can practice equanimity, in both positive and negative moments, and our happiness is likely to expand. And we can teach our children to be alert to watching and waiting when intense feelings come. If they have trained their concentration by noting what's going on in the present moment, they can also watch their feelings.

Strengthening the Happiness Muscles: Our Children and Ourselves

As caring parents we want happiness for our children. We enjoy the close moments and want to extend them. Many of us know how to be friends with our children and to support their desires and talents. But you've seen repeatedly that getting stuck in the box of being special causes great suffering for children, teens, and young adults. A special self weakens their happiness muscles as well as the autonomy muscles they'll need to stand on their own. Throughout the book I have suggested a variety of practical changes we can make in our attitudes and relationships to bring about a new kind of self-confidence in our children.

I know that changing your parenting style is hard. Changing our habits in relating to anyone sometimes seems impossible. With your kids, though, the good news is that just by virtue of being kids, they can accept change. Their bodies, their brains, their environments, and their experiences are rapidly evolving all the time. Just think what a different creature an infant is from a toddler, a toddler from a grade-school child, and that grade-school child from a teenager. Much of what this book has recommended will require a change in your interactions with your own and others' children. That change is likely to be easier for them than for you.

My friend Shannon told me of a conversation she had with another mother about changing her style of parenting. Stephanie came from an economically privileged but emotionally challenging background. She left her highly skilled career when the third of her five children was born and threw herself wholeheartedly into child rearing. Stephanie made sure that every need was met—be it for hugs and kisses for a bruised knee or bruised ego, or for trips to Europe to celebrate important milestones. She was also quick to praise her children for their accomplishments. Artwork was displayed, good grades richly rewarded, special talents nourished and upheld. Then Stephanie read an article in a newsmagazine about the effects of overpraising and indulging children. She began to profoundly rethink her approach to her five children.

She first talked with her husband about her concerns. They agreed that they both needed to scale back the amount of praise they gave their children. They also decided to change what they were unconsciously emphasizing—that their children were special. After they had their basic game plan, they called a family meeting, during which they sat all the kids down and told them what they were changing and why. They told them that they still loved each of them and always would, but that Mom and Dad would no longer be their cheerleaders. They emphasized that they wanted their kids to be happy and successful, and that they thought the best way of accomplishing this was by helping the kids build better connections to each other and to their larger community.

Stephanie and her husband worked hard at changing the way they spoke to and acted toward their children, and they are still making adjustments. But what Stephanie found surprising was how easily the children adapted. In fact all of them have begun to jokingly correct her when she slips into her old habits.

As a parent you are the leader. You have the power to make changes in your parenting, whether your child is one or twenty-one. Your words and actions will influence a great deal more of your child's developing humanity than you may believe. Do not assume that you and your children are equals or that everyone's point of view is equally valid. A family is not a democracy. Instead guide your child by rule and example to become a well-mannered, kind, autonomous adult with a sound conscience. Over the long years of your child's dependency, that's a complex and demanding task. Your job is not to be your child's best friend, but rather to prepare him to have a fulfilling life of his own.

Your first responsibility is to teach your child how to become a contributing member of a family, community, society, and species. Remember the importance of emotional intelligence (self-awareness, impulse control, empathy with others) for happiness and success, especially in leadership, relationships, groups, and creativity. Help your child use the six practices of being ordinary and the skills of emotional intelligence.

Cultivating, remembering, and talking about the six practices for being ordinary will put individual success and achievement into perspective. When our children succeed at gaining privilege or status, their accomplishments depend on the involvements and sacrifices of many others in addition to themselves. All accomplishments are truly and deeply shared. When we feel these connections, we find it easier to embrace and experience success—our own and others'—in an unself-conscious way. This increases our happiness.

As I emphasized in chapter seven, you can expand your children's appreciation for life by helping them become sensitive to its passages—to birth, aging, illness, and death. Good health is a temporary state for all of us. When we spend time visiting or caring for someone who is ill, we become aware of our good fortune in temporarily feeling good. All of the ways in which we share with others in the common struggles and distress of our lives can increase our generosity, gratitude, and trust—the foundations for our own happiness.

Trust and Happiness

Close to my home is a private military college, established in 1819, that educates a corps of cadets and a population of civilian students. I became interested in Norwich University because it actively promotes good manners and guiding values. In working as a consultant on their campuswide initiative to develop emotionally intelligent leadership skills (across all of the populations: students, faculty, staff, administration), I have learned a great deal about myself, as well as others, in regard to the demands that leadership makes on us as a character trait. To cultivate and foster our inherent leadership skills (to make things happen in groups, while maintaining good relations with each other), we have to keep others constantly in mind.

When I interviewed Martha Mathis, dean of students at Norwich, in my research for this book, I hadn't yet become a consultant at the university. Dean Mathis is a slender, attractive, middle-aged woman with a kind manner, a sparkle in her eye, and a way of tilting her head sideways as if to say "Really? Do you believe that?"

When I began my conversation with Dean Mathis, I assumed that certain habits among Norwich students would have shifted over the past five to ten years—for instance, feelings of entitlement and bad manners—in much the same ways I had heard about at other colleges. When I asked Martha about it, she tilted her head and replied, "Well, I think Norwich is a different place. So much of our roots and foundation is based on a serious honor code and guiding values. We promote certain values at a higher value, if you will, probably more than academics. When you buy into Norwich, you buy into a pretty strict code of ethics." She continued: "Over the years, the students who have had the best chance of succeeding here are those with a sound moral code.

The ones who will succeed are accustomed to having a lot of people asking them a lot of questions and knowing how to answer politely."

When I asked again if things had changed in the recent decade or so, she said, "Well, I think it's changed a little bit. The parents are more engaged now, because they are paying so much for the education here. They feel more ownership, which I welcome." I wondered about problems with helicopter parents, and Dean Mathis shrugged and said, "I think it's an asset. I never categorize them that way." In my long and pleasant conversation with Martha Mathis, I realized that I was encountering an environment in which good manners and good character were expected, part of the deal. Parents and kids knew in coming here that the skills of focusing away from self, and toward duty, community, and others, would be emphasized.

Dean Mathis reminded me that succeeding at Norwich was "not wrapped up in privilege. It's more wrapped up in morals and interdependence." I was surprised to hear that last word and responded by asking, "Caring for your community?" and she said, "Yeah. I like the fact that my purse and my credit cards are lying in my car, as we speak, and my keys are in the ignition. I like that. There's something to be said when you can count on the social fabric of your community. And so when I have contact with a student here, when a student comes to the dean's office, I am not immediately suspicious. We might get there, but that's not where I start."

Coming away from my interview with Dean Mathis and studying the guiding values of Norwich, I was intrigued. From my personal background and my long career in doing couples therapy, I know that our trust in one another is the foundation for our happiest experiences. When we fundamentally believe that those we depend on—our parents, friends, partners, and ourselves—can be trusted, we are immediately happier and more relaxed. If you think about this for a moment, you know that it is the reason character and virtue matter more than talent and provide us with the base for developing our gifts.

Accepting Ourselves as We Are

In the first chapter, we heard Adrienne, in her young thirties, say that her goal was "not to sink into this darkness." We've learned that this darkness is the self-esteem trap of negative self-absorption: anxiety, fears of humiliation, restlessness, and shame that are the unfortunate companions of our exaggerated expectations for ourselves and our lives. What's it like to be free from the self-esteem trap?

First and foremost, it's always a work in progress. We don't arrive at self-acceptance and then just live there. Every day we engage anew with our relationships and ourselves, drawing on the resilience that comes from overcoming adversity and solving problems; the discipline of a good conscience and virtues; the self-determination and self-reliance of our autonomy; the practice of being ordinary; and an ever-increasing openness to our interdependence through empathy, love, compassion, and spirituality.

As parents we discover that teaching and showing our children the path to self-acceptance enriches our opportunities for the same. This book has repeatedly described and illustrated the way to a new kind of self-confidence that is not based on idealized expectations for ourselves or others. When we feel poised to attack ourselves for not meeting some ideal expectations—whether we are children, teens, or adults—we pause, then look for a more realistic and compassionate approach. Knowing that difficulties and disappointments, as well as pain and illness, are a part of life, we no longer expect that we can keep these contractive experiences entirely away from us. Rather we see how we can learn from them, have a sense of humor about them, and not expect to do even these perfectly.

We learn to hold ourselves in mind with kindness, as fragile human beings who have limitations of all sorts. We become compassionate for ourselves when we notice that we are feeling pressured by impossible ideals and concentrate, with equanimity, on allowing the feelings to move through us. Then we try to increase our self-knowledge by noting our unhelpful emotional habits: the ways in which we have learned to defend ourselves by rationalizing or attacking our actions and thoughts. We hold all of this in mind with compassion, and say or do something to embrace the whole mess. Personally, I take a moment to value my weaknesses, limitations, or mistakes as reminders of my humanity.

To work against our habits of negative self-absorption and exaggerated expectations, we keep certain things in mind, teaching our children to do the same. First we keep in mind those on whom we immediately depend—ourselves, those in the room with us at any moment, and those who are in close relationship with us. Our conversation and our action should support our bonds with these people—not necessarily agreeing with them, but holding in mind their desires and vulnerabilities. When we speak or act, we maintain respect for ourselves and the others with whom we are relating.

It's also helpful to follow a simple speech practice that can be taught to children. When you are speaking at times of conflict or with negative feelings and need to step back and reflect, or when you otherwise remember to do so, ask yourself if what you are about to say is (1) truthful, (2) kind, and (3) necessary. If it is, then speak. If not, try again. Don't expect to do this perfectly, but hold it as a general guideline and occasionally review it aloud with your children.[8]

Remind yourself (and your children) to take a moment before speaking to check in with your thoughts, feelings, attitudes, and empathy with others in the room. After speaking or acting, you can look back and see what has emerged from the interchange. Your self-acceptance automatically increases when you pay attention to what's going on with others, because doing this reminds you that you are never alone and can rely on others. If you speak poorly or hurt someone, you can apologize and try again. There is no ideal end in this process.

Having this capacity to repeatedly check in with themselves and accept themselves with compassion and kindness will gradually make your children grateful for their faults, weaknesses, and limitations, even their bad habits. Bad habits can become our teachers. When we stumble upon them, as we must, we always learn from them, whether we are alone or with others. Our mistakes, too, are friendly companions when they make us laugh and see ourselves more clearly. And so we can enjoy our own company no matter how we are functioning.

Our self-compassion increases our autonomy because we are less afraid of challenges and adversity. Whatever comes up, we'll find a way to respond to and learn from it. When we are kind even in our self-criticism, we can become more open, flexible, and courageous in moving toward relationships, creativity, and leadership on one hand, and pain and adversity on the other. We become confident that we can work with both our strengths and our weaknesses and get help when we need it, not pushing ourselves beyond our internal resources.

Teaching our children these relational skills and modeling the behaviors, we can banish the pressures and negativity of the self-esteem trap and embrace happiness when it strikes. Eventually we may find that we enjoy our own company as much as we enjoy the company of others, rarely distinguishing ourselves very sharply from others, except as it's necessary to consider differences and limitations. With compassion and care turned inward and outward, we find that the warmth of love is always available because we can bring it to ourselves.

Acknowledgments

Of course this book could not exist without the many interviews that provide its foundation. And so first I want to thank each and every person I interviewed—both named and unnamed. I collected thousands of pages of interview transcripts in preparing to write the book. Every person who participated in helping me investigate the self-esteem trap was generous, articulate, and insightful. I learned and developed my ideas anew with each interview. Thank you all.

Second, I want to thank my own psychotherapy clients, who first brought to my attention the many forms of suffering that this book tries to ameliorate. My clients' stories and questions are challenging, fascinating, and inspiring beyond what outsiders might imagine; similarly, their openheartedness and generosity are always remarkable. I would not have written this book had I not been meeting with mothers, fathers, and young adults who clearly needed a new perspective on the problem of self-importance in child rearing and everyday family life. My experiences with my clients in psychotherapy and psychoanalysis have been my major teachers in the field of psychology for more than two decades. It is a privilege to have the personal view that I have into people's lives. I am forever grateful.

The specific people who provided intelligent critiques and scholarly help have also been invaluable. Sharon Broll, my personal editor, has gone well beyond anything that could be called duty for this book. From the inception she raised questions and helped me order my thoughts. Eventually she found the thread of sequencing that made sense of my ideas, and helped me tighten the structure while trimming the fat off my prose. I loved every minute of the process. Sharon has assisted me on several books, and I cannot acknowledge her contribution too highly.

My literary agent, Jill Kneerim, has been a role model as a human being as well as an expert guide through the publishing world. Without her encouragement and good humor, I would have been lost. She is a true friend.

In the earliest stages of preparation, I was ably assisted by Kristy Mamchur, who helped with scholarly research and followed leads from magazine and journal articles. Kristy questioned, probed, and came along on many a conceptual journey in my initial inquiries about our cultural overfocus on the self and its consequences. I cannot thank you enough, Kristy.

Lisa Condon then took the baton from Kristy and finished the race by planning and writing the scholarly endnotes. Lisa was thoughtful and efficient in her work and completed her tasks in an admirably autonomous way. Thank you so much for all that you added to this book, Lisa.

My word-processing assistant, Deb Wells, has also been on my book-writing team for many years now. She is able, always precise, and unbelievably dedicated. On several occasions Deb made special trips to pick up or deliver the manuscript so that we could meet deadlines. Her efforts on my behalf have been truly extraordinary.

Tracy Behar, my editor at Little, Brown, has been a confident and efficient guide in putting together the final product. She also helped me see what was more and less important in the stories I wanted to tell. It has been a pleasure to work with her.

And finally, this book could not have been written without my long and rich exposure to the Buddhadharma—the teachings of the Buddha and his followers. For more than thirty years, Buddhism has, in myriad ways, played a central role in my understanding of why and how we suffer from overemphasizing the individual self in our perceptions and feelings. In these recent years, I have been especially grateful to have had the guidance of Shinzen Young in the practice of Vipassana, and in earlier decades, of Philip Kapleau Roshi in the practice of Zen.

Of course I forever cherish the friendship and help of my husband, Ed Epstein, who encourages and provides emotional support for my writing. Together we have been partners and parents and have struggled in all of the ways I write about here. Working on this particular book, I spent countless hours questioning and reviewing with Ed various aspects and episodes of our roles in raising our three children. Ed accompanied me on a couple of the longest interviews. These encounters were much enriched by the conversations that we had before and after. As always, I am deeply grateful for Ed's friendship and humor.

In the end, however, I take full responsibility for what I have written here, and I hope that it is helpful in freeing us all from the self-esteem trap.

Notes

Introduction

1. For a thorough discussion of this cultural trend, see, for example, Madeline Levine, *The Price of Privilege: How Parental Pressure and Material Advantage Are Creating a Generation of Disconnected and Unhappy Kids* (New York: HarperCollins, 2006) and Jean M. Twenge, *Generation Me: Why Today's Young Americans Are More Confident, Assertive, Entitled—and More Miserable Than Ever Before* (New York: Free Press, 2006).

2. See Twenge, *Generation Me,* chapter two, for a socio-historical overview of the shift toward promoting self-esteem in parenting and education in the 1970s and 1980s.

3. For instance: Alan Eisenstock, *The Kindergarten Wars: The Battle to Get Into America's Best Private Schools* (New York: Warner, 2006); John Hewitt, *The Myth of Self-Esteem: Finding Happiness and Solving Problems in America* (New York: St. Martin's, 1998); Dan Kindlon, *Too Much of a Good Thing: Raising Children of Character in an Indulgent Age* (New York: Mirimax, 2001); Levine, *The Price of Privilege;* Christie Mellor, *The Three-Martini Playdate: A Practical Guide to Happy Parenting* (San Francisco: Chronicle, 2004); Alissa Quart, *Hothouse Kids: The Dilemma of the Gifted Child* (New York: Penguin, 2006); Alexandra Robbins, *The Overachievers: The Secret Lives of Driven Kids* (New York: Hyperion, 2006); and Twenge, *Generation Me.*

4. For example, see P. J. Watson, Tracy Little, and Michael D. Biderman, "Narcissism and Parenting Styles," *Psychoanalytic Psychology* 9 (1992): 231.

5. In addition, a number of books I have written deal with the interaction between sociocultural context and the psychology of the individual. For instance, see Polly Young-Eisendrath and Florence Wiedemann, *Female Authority: Empowering Women Through Psychotherapy* (New York: Guilford Press, 1987); Polly Young-Eisendrath, *You're Not What I Expected: Learning to Love the Opposite Sex* (New York: William Morrow, 1993); Polly Young-Eisendrath, *Gender and Desire: Uncursing Pandora* (College Station: Texas A&M University Press, 1997); and Polly Young-Eisendrath, *Women and Desire: Beyond Wanting to Be Wanted* (New York: Three Rivers Press, 1999).

6. For a summary of several research papers on brain development during adolescence, see National Institutes of Health, National Institute of Mental Health, *Teenage Brain: A Work in Progress*, NIH Publication No. 01-4929, 2001.

7. John K. Rosemond agrees with me in viewing symptoms that are commonly labeled as "attention deficit" as being the result of a shift in parenting from a "realistic" to an "idealistic" point of view. See John K. Rosemond, "The Diseasing of America's Children: The Politics of Diagnosis," in *Destructive Trends in Mental Health: The Well-Intentioned Path to Harm*, eds. R. H. Wright and N. A. Cummings (New York: Routledge, 2005).

8. Twenge, *Generation Me*, 1.

9. See Twenge, *Generation Me*, 5.

10. Robert Bellah et al., *Habits of the Heart: Individualism and Commitment in American Life* (New York: Harper and Row, 1985), 84.

11. See Mark Epstein, for instance, *Going to Pieces Without Falling Apart: A Buddhist Perspective on Wholeness* (New York: Broadway Books, 1998), for a discussion of the ways in which striving to attain material goods and status impedes true happiness. Also see Paul R. Fulton and Ronald D. Siegel, "Buddhist and Western Psychology: Seeking Common Ground," in *Mindfulness and Psychotherapy*, eds. C. K. Germer, R. D. Siegel, and P. R. Fulton (New York: Guilford Press, 2005), 40–42, for an explanation of the Buddhist view that seeing the self as substantial and fixed leads to suffering.

12. See Sharon Lamb and Lyn Mikel Brown, *Packaging Girlhood: Rescuing Our Daughters from Marketers' Schemes* (New York: St. Martin's, 2006); Young-Eisendrath, *Gender and Desire;* and Young-Eisendrath, *Women and Desire,* for a discussion of the ways in which being female is linked to particular social values.

13. See William Pollack, *Real Boys: Rescuing Our Sons from the Myths of Boyhood* (New York: Owl Books, 1999), for a discussion of the ways in which being male is linked to particular social values.

14. Young-Eisendrath, *Women and Desire.*

15. See Annette Lareau, for example, *Unequal Childhoods: Class, Race, and Family Life* (Berkeley: University of California Press, 2003).

Chapter One: The Trouble with Being Special

1. A number of studies have found increased rates of various emotional disorders in current versus past generations. For instance, lifetime rates of major depression in people born before 1915 are 1 percent to 2 percent (see P. J. Wickramaratne et al., "Age, Period, and Cohort Effects on the Risk of Major Depression: Results from Five United States Communities," *Journal of Clinical Epidemiology* 42 [1989]: 333–43), whereas one 1990s study found that 21 percent of teens had already had a major depressive episode (see P. M. Lewinsohn et al., "Age-Cohort Changes in the Lifetime Occurrence of Depression and Other Mental Disorders," *Journal of Abnormal Psychology* 102 [1993]: 110–20). Also, several studies have found evidence of increased narcissism in the current generation. One study found that the number of teens endorsing the item "I am an important person" had increased from 12 percent in the early 1950s to 80 percent in the late 1980s (see C. R. Newson, "Changes in Adolescent Response Patterns on the MMPI/MMPI-A Across Four Decades," *Journal of Personality Assessment* 81 [2003]: 74–84). In addition, a 2002 survey found that age was related to a higher score on the Narcissistic Personality Inventory, with people under thirty-five years old having the highest scores (see Joshua Foster, Keith Campbell, and Jean Twenge, "Individual Differences in Narcissism: Inflated Self-Views Across the Lifespan and Around the World," *Journal of Research in Personality* 37 [2002]: 469–86).

2. For instance, a number of articles have been written about young people expecting to reap the benefits of a career before putting in

their time as an employee. See Martha Irvine, "Age of 'Entitlement' Changes Rules: Generation of Workers Demand More from Workplace," *Grand Rapids Press,* July 3, 2005, section H.

3. See, for example, Rosemond, "The Diseasing of America's Children," in *Destructive Trends in Mental Health,* eds. Wright and Cummings. Other chapters in this book are also relevant to a critique of biological reasoning about development.

4. See Richard C. Lewontin, *Biology and Ideology: The Doctrine of DNA* (Toronto: House of Anansi Press, 1991), for a critique of the authority of science. Lewontin argues that instead of being objective and outside the realm of social bias, science is in fact socially mediated, and that it serves social, political, and economic agendas.

5. As an example of how rapidly this trend in medicating children has increased, the number of children on psychiatric medications tripled between 1987 and 1997. See Julie M. Zito et al., "Psychotropic Practice Patterns for Youth: A Ten-Year Perspective," *Archives of Pediatrics and Adolescent Medicine* 157 (2003): 17–25.

6. For other accounts of children displaying inappropriate social control, see Judith Warner, *Perfect Madness: Motherhood in the Age of Anxiety* (New York: Riverhead Books, 2005); Mellor, *The Three-Martini Playdate;* and Judith Warner, "Kids Gone Wild," *New York Times,* November 27, 2005, Week in Review section.

7. For other discussions on the concept of a self-conscious self, see Polly Young-Eisendrath and James Hall, *Jung's Self Psychology: A Constructivist Perspective* (New York: Guilford Press, 1991); Charles Taylor, *The Sources of the Self: The Making of Modern Identity* (Cambridge, MA: Harvard University Press, 1989); Robert Kegan, *The Evolving Self: Problem and Process in Human Development* (Cambridge, MA: Harvard University Press, 1982); and Joseph LeDoux, *The Synaptic Self: How Our Brains Become Who We Are* (New York: Viking, 2002).

8. See Rom Harré, *Personal Being: A Theory for Individual Psychology* (Cambridge, MA: Harvard University Press, 1986).

9. For examples, see Polly Young-Eisendrath and Terence Dawson, eds., *The Cambridge Companion to Jung* (Cambridge, England: Cambridge University Press, 1997).

10. For example, see Erik Erikson, *Childhood and Society* (New York: W. W. Norton, 1964, 1986, 1993).

11. See, for instance, John Bowlby, *Attachment,* vol. 1 of *Attachment and Loss* (New York: Basic Books, 1969). A whole body of work and research has developed in the past forty years around the concept of attachment relationships. See also note 2 in chapter eight.

12. *Webster's II New College Dictionary,* 2nd ed. (Boston: Houghton Mifflin, 1999).

13. See Alfie Kohn, *Unconditional Parenting: Moving from Rewards and Punishments to Love and Reason* (New York: Atria Books, 2005), and Karen K. Burhans and Carol S. Dweck, "Helplessness in Early Childhood: The Role of Contingent Worth," *Child Development* 66 (1995): 1719.

14. See Levine, *The Price of Privilege.*

15. The literature on Buddhism is quite extensive. For a very concise introduction to Buddhism, see Ruben L. F. Habito, *Experiencing Buddhism: Ways of Wisdom and Compassion* (Maryknoll, NY: Orbis Books, 2005), or visit the Web site www.shinzen.org. For an overview of the various schools of psychoanalytic psychology, see Stephen A. Mitchell and Margaret J. Black, *Freud and Beyond: A History of Modern Psychoanalytic Thought* (New York: Basic Books, 1995).

16. For more on autonomy as self-determination and self-governance, see Young-Eisendrath, *Gender and Desire.*

17. For an explanation of this central teaching of Buddhism (that discontent and adversity are an inevitable part of life), see the Dalai Lama, *The Four Noble Truths* (London: Thorsons, 1997), and Rob Nairn, *What Is Meditation?: Buddhism for Everyone* (Boston: Shambhala, 2000).

18. Stephen S. Hall, "The Older-and-Wiser Hypothesis," *New York Times Magazine,* May 6, 2007.

19. See Monika Ardelt, "Social Crisis and Individual Growth: The Long-term Effects of the Great Depression," *Journal of Aging Studies* 12 (1998): 291; D. A. Kramer, "Wisdom as a Classical Source of Human Strength: Conceptualization and Empirical Inquiry," *Journal of Social and Clinical Psychology* 19 (2000): 83; Virginia E. O'Leary and Jeanette R. Ickovics, "Resilience and Thriving in Response to Challenge: An Opportunity for a Paradigm Shift in Women's Health," *Women's Health: Research on Gender, Behavior, and Policy* 1 (1995): 121; Michael Rutter, "Psychosocial Resilience and Proactive Mechanisms," *American*

Journal of Orthopsychiatry 57 (1987): 316; and Michele M. Tugade and Barbara L. Fredrickson, "Resilient Individuals Use Positive Emotions to Bounce Back from Negative Emotional Experiences," *Journal of Personality and Social Psychology* 86 (2004): 320.

Chapter Two: The Roots of the Problem

1. See Jonathan D. Glatter, "To: Professor@University.edu; Subject: Why It's All About Me," *New York Times,* February 12, 2006, Education section, and Twenge, *Generation Me,* 28–29.
2. Margaret Mead commented on the experience of the isolated nuclear family of the 1950s and 1960s in her famous quote "Nobody has ever before asked the nuclear family to live all by itself in a box the way we do. With no relatives, no support, we've put it in an impossible situation." See *Columbia World of Quotations,* eds. Robert Andrews, Mary Briggs, and Michael Seidel (New York: Columbia University Press, 1996), www.bartleby.com/66/78/ 38578.html.
3. See, for example, Alice Miller, *The Drama of the Gifted Child: The Search for the True Self* (New York: HarperCollins, 1996).
4. See Christopher Lasch, *The Culture of Narcissism* (New York: W. W. Norton, 1979).
5. Thomas A. Harris, *I'm OK — You're OK: A Practical Guide to Transactional Analysis* (New York: Harper and Row, 1969).
6. In general the term "laissez-faire parenting" refers to a permissive style of parenting that emphasizes children's self-expression, with a minimum of guidance, discipline, or control. For a description of laissez-faire parenting, see John Gottman, *Raising an Emotionally Intelligent Child: The Heart of Parenting* (New York: Fireside, 1997). Research on parenting styles has found that children of permissive parents were more impulsive, disobedient, and demanding than children raised with other parenting styles. See Diana Baumrind, "Rearing Competent Children," in *Child Development Today and Tomorrow,* ed. William Damon (San Francisco: Jossey-Bass, 1989), 349.
7. The term "helicopter parenting" is widely used in academic settings and refers to parents who are overinvolved with their children, particularly in academic and career matters. See "Helicopter Parents Reconsidered," www.collegeboard.com/parents/plan/getting-

ready/155044.html, and Barbara Kantrowitz and Peg Tyre, "The Fine Art of Letting Go," *Newsweek*, May 22, 2006.

8. Kindlon, *Too Much of a Good Thing*, xi.

9. Warner, *Perfect Madness*, 226.

10. Lee Carroll and Jan Tober, *The Indigo Children: The New Kids Have Arrived* (Carlsbad, CA: Light Technology Publications, 1999).

11. In 2006 a documentary called *The Indigo Evolution* was released, describing the Indigo movement (see www.indigoevolution.com). Newspaper articles have been written about this movement as well; for example, see John Leland, "Are They Here to Save the World?" *New York Times*, January 12, 2006, Health section.

Chapter Three: The Importance of Adversity

1. For more information about Miss Hall's School for Girls, see their Web site at www.misshalls.org.

2. See Judy B. Garber, N. S. Robinson, and D. Valentiner, "The Relationship Between Parenting Style and Adolescent Depression: Self-Worth as a Mediator," *Journal of Adolescent Research* 12 (1997): 12; and Brian K. Barber and Elizabeth L. Harmon, "Violating the Self: Parental Psychological Control of Children and Adolescents," in *Intrusive Parenting: How Psychological Control Affects Children and Adolescents*, ed. Brian K. Barber (Washington, DC: American Psychological Association, 2002), 15.

3. In his book *Emerging Adulthood,* Jeffrey J. Arnett describes the shift in the past few decades to a delayed adulthood. For instance, he notes that in the 1970s, a typical twenty-one-year-old was likely to have completed formal education, be married, be starting a family, and have settled into a career, whereas today, individuals are likely to be in their late twenties or older before settling into any one of these milestones of adulthood. See *Emerging Adulthood: The Winding Road from the Late Teens to the Twenties* (New York: Oxford University Press, 2004).

4. In 2005 a government survey found that 8.3 percent of sixteen-to-seventeen-year-olds and 19.8 percent of eighteen-to-twenty-year-olds had driven while intoxicated at least once during the past year. See U.S. Department of Health and Human Services, "2005 Survey on Drug Use and Health: National Results," Office of Applied Studies, SAMHSA, www.oas.samhsa.gov/NSDUH/2k5NSDUH/2k5results.htm#Ch3.

5. For more information about family meetings, including ideas about how to do family meetings, see Kristen Zolten and Nicholas Long, "Family Meetings," Center for Effective Parenting, Arkansas State PIRC, 1997, www.parenting-ed.org/parenting-handouts. htm, and Elaine Hightower and Betsy Riley, *Our Family Meeting Book: Fun and Easy Ways to Manage Time, Build Communication, and Share Responsibility Week by Week* (Minneapolis: Free Spirit, 2002).

6. Dalai Lama, *The Four Noble Truths.*

7. One study of self-injury on college campuses found that 17 percent of students surveyed engaged in self-injury, and 75 percent of those who self-injured did so repeatedly. The authors of this study also noted that there are more than four hundred message boards on the Internet geared toward sharing experiences of self-injury. See Joan J. Brumberg, "Are We Facing an Epidemic of Self-Injury?" *Chronicle of Higher Education* 53 (2006): B6.

8. See the story of Flint and Flo in Jane Goodall, *The Chimpanzees of Gombe: Patterns of Behavior* (Boston: Harvard University Press, 1986).

9. Neff, Hsieh, and Dejitterat studied the relationship between self-compassion and reactions to academic failure. They found that self-compassion was related to a tendency to accept getting a bad grade and to respond by trying to improve academically. In other words, self-compassion seemed to enable students to take responsibility for their poor grades and to integrate this failure into their sense of self without feeling overwhelmed by it. See Kristen Neff, Ya-Ping Hsieh, and Kullaya Dejitterat, "Self-Compassion, Achievement Goals, and Coping with Academic Failure," *Self and Identity* 2 (2005): 263–87.

10. See David Hilfiker, *Healing the Wounds: A Doctor Looks at His Work* (New York: Pantheon, 1985), and David Hilfiker, *Not All of Us Are Saints: A Doctor's Journey with the Poor* (New York: Ballantine, 1994).

11. David Hilfiker, "Seeing Poverty After Katrina," interview by Krista Tippett, *Speaking of Faith,* National Public Radio, August 24, 2006.

12. See Karin Hilfiker, "Tears of Grief, Tears of Joy," *With,* December 1991: 9.

Chapter Four: The Necessity of Conscience and Virtue

1. See "Do Ethics Still Matter?: Lichtman/Zobgy Poll of Young Americans Say 'Yes, But . . . .' " Zogby International, May 9, 2005, www.zogby.com/news/ReadNews.dbm?ID=991.

2. See Josephson Institute of Ethics, "2004 Josephson Institute Report Card on Ethics of American Youth: Part One—Integrity," www.josephsoninstitute.org/Survey2004/2004reportcard-press release.htm.

3. For instance, the Enron scandal (see Harry Maurer, "Enron: Guilty, Guilty, Guilty," *Business Week,* June 12, 2006) and the leaking of the identity of undercover CIA officer Valerie Plame (see Jim Vandehei, "Probe Focuses on Rove's Testimony; As He Wraps Up, Special Counsel Asking if Deputy Chief of Staff Lied About Conversation," *Houston Chronicle,* May 8, 2006) are examples of recent, high-profile, "real world" people involved in unethical behavior.

4. See page 3 of "2004 Josephson Institute Report Card."

5. See Steve Farkas and Jean Johnson, with Ann Duffett and Kathleen Collins, "Aggravating Circumstances: A Status Report on Rudeness in America," Public Agenda, 2002, www.publicagenda.org/specials/civility/civility4.htm.

6. See Alex P. Kellogg, "Facing more, and Possibly Pickier Students, Colleges Renovate and Add Housing," *Chronicle of Higher Education,* October 19, 2001, for a report on the increased demand for single rooms and more amenities (e.g., free parking spaces, more living space, increased privacy) in campus housing. Kellogg cites several college surveys that found that wanting a single room was a top reason that students chose to attend another school, and he notes that the majority of college students have never shared a bedroom with a sibling, and are used to having their own room, television, computer, and phone. Another newspaper article reports that according to a college administrator's informal survey of incoming freshmen, only about five out of two hundred students say they have ever shared a room with a sibling (see Karen G. Goff, "Lessons in Life: Sharing Space; Rules Help as Children Compromise," *Washington Times,* October 10, 2004, section D).

7. My discussion and analysis of Robert Tulloch and James Parker is

partly based on information I integrated from reading *Judgment Ridge,* as well as from interviewing psychiatrist Andrew Pomerantz and from reading a number of newspaper articles that were printed at the time of the Dartmouth murders. See Dick Lehr and Mitchell Zuckoff, *Judgment Ridge: The True Story Behind the Dartmouth Murders* (New York: HarperCollins, 2003).

8. All of the quotes in this paragraph are found on page 150 of Lehr and Zuckoff, *Judgment Ridge.*

9. Ibid., 150.

10. In the *Diagnostic and Statistical Manual of Mental Disorders (DSM-IV-TR),* the term Antisocial Personality Disorder is used to describe someone who is more commonly described as a "psychopath." In the *DSM-IV-TR,* antisocial personality disorder is one of a cluster of disorders, in which an individual demonstrates significant disregard for the rights of others and may be aggressive, impulsive, and lack remorse for wrongdoing. See *Diagnostic and Statistical Manual of Mental Disorders, 4th Edition, Text Revision,* ed. Michael B. First (Washington, DC: American Psychiatric Publishing, 2000).

    Narcissistic Personality Disorder is in the same cluster of personality disorders as is Antisocial Personality Disorder. Although these two diagnoses are similar in terms of lacking empathy and concern for others, they differ in terms of the specific patterns of behavior. Narcissistic Personality Disorder is characterized by a pattern of significant self-importance, fantasies of unrealistic success, need for constant admiration, sense of entitlement, and using others to meet one's own needs. See *DSM-IV-TR.*

11. *Webster's II New College Dictionary.*

12. For a general reference on virtue, see Christopher Peterson and Martin E. P. Seligman, *Character Strengths and Virtues: A Handbook and Classification* (New York: American Psychological Association and Oxford University Press, 2004).

13. See, for example, Nagapriya, *Exploring Karma and Rebirth* (Birmingham, UK: Windhorse, 2005).

14. Peterson and Seligman, *Character Strengths and Virtues,* 119.

15. In this study, students were asked to look at Card #1 of the Thematic Apperception Test. See David Ephraim, "A Psychocultural Approach to TAT Scoring," in *Handbook of Cross-Cultural and Multicultural Personality Assessment,* ed. R. H. Dana (Mahwaw, NJ: Lawrence Erlbaum, 2000), 427.

16. Ibid., 432.

17. Ibid., 433, for both quotes from Japanese students.

18. Peterson and Seligman, *Character Strengths and Virtues,* 229.

19. Jean Piaget, *The Moral Judgment of the Child* (New York: Free Press Paperbacks, 1997), 147.

20. In a study on postadolescent brain development, researchers found that in late adolescence the human brain undergoes significant development in the frontal lobes, which are responsible for cognitive processing and "executive" functions such as impulse control, planning, and reasoning. See Elizabeth Sowell et al., "In Vivo Evidence for Post-Adolescent Brain Maturation in Frontal and Striatal Regions," *Nature Neuroscience* 2 (1999): 859–61.

21. Gigi Marks is an assistant professor of writing at the School of Humanities and Sciences, Ithaca College, in Ithaca, New York.

22. Estimates of infidelity among late adolescents range from 20 percent to 64 percent. See S. Shirley Feldman and Elizabeth Cauffman, "Sexual Betrayal Among Late Adolescents: Perspectives of the Perpetrator and the Aggrieved," *Journal of Youth and Adolescence* 28 (1999): 235–58, and Catherine M. Grello, Deborah P. Welsh, and Melinda S. Harper, "No Strings Attached: The Nature of Casual Sex in College Students," *Journal of Sex Research* 43 (2006): 255–67.

Chapter Five: Autonomy and Emotional Maturity

1. Citing U.S. Census Bureau statistics, a newspaper article from 2006 states that the number of eighteen-to-thirty-four-year-olds returning to live at home has increased 48 percent since 1970. See Suzette Hackney, "More Adult Children Returning to the Nest: It's a Cultural Custom for Some and a Financial Need for Others," *Houston Chronicle,* June 19, 2006, Business section.

2. The National Institute of Mental Health (NIMH) has published an overview of research on brain development during adolescence. This paper summarizes current research showing that during the teenage years, the brain undergoes significant developmental changes that are related to the maturation of cognitive processes. See National Institutes of Health, *Teenage Brain.*

3. David Elkind, "Egocentrism in Adolescence," in *Readings in Developmental Psychology,* 2nd ed., eds. Judith Krieger Gardner and Ed Gardner (Reading, MA: Addison-Wesley, 1978), 1025–33.

4. Journalists and researchers have noted that today's youth, having

been raised with an emphasis on being special, feel entitled to material rewards and praise. For example, in an Associated Press article from 2005, journalist Martha Irvine refers to today's youth as the "Entitlement Generation" and notes that they expect high salaries and promotions without putting in time or effort (see Martha Irvine, "Young Labeled 'Entitlement Generation,'" Associated Press, June 26, 2005, www.bizyahoo.com/ap/050626/the_entitlement_generation.html2.v3). In addition, research has shown that people in the current generation (i.e., under age thirty-five) score higher on the Narcissistic Personality Inventory (see Foster et al., "Individual Differences in Narcissism").

5. For a detailed account of Andrew's own psychotherapy and self-reflections, see "Andrew: Insecurity, Inferiority, Social Anxiety, and Submissiveness," in Joseph Schachter, ed., *Transforming Lives: Analyst and Patient View the Power of Psychoanalytic Treatment* (New York: Jason Aronson, 2005), 127–48.

6. Twenge, *Generation Me*, 78.

7. Ibid., 105.

8. Ibid., 106.

9. Ibid., 107.

10. Schachter, "Andrew: Insecurity, Inferiority," 141–42.

11. Ibid., 142.

12. For more information about the concept of superego, see Hans Blum, "Superego Formation, Adolescent Transformation, and Adult Neurosis," *Journal of the Psychoanalytic Association* 33 (1985): 887; Hans W. Loewald, "Some Instinctual Manifestations of Superego Formation," *Annual of Psychoanalysis* 1 (1973): 104; and David Milrod, "The Superego: Its Formation, Structure, and Functioning," *Psychoanalytic Study of the Child* 57 (2002): 131.

13. Schachter, "Andrew: Insecurity, Inferiority," 143.

14. Ibid., 140.

15. For research on the influence of the parent-child relationship on brain development, see William T. Greenough and James E. Black, "Induction of Brain Structure by Experience: Substrates for Cognitive Development," in *Minnesota Symposia on Child Psychology: Development Neuroscience*, vol. 24, eds. M. R. Gunnar and C. A. Nelson (Hillsdale, NJ: Lawrence Erlbaum, 1997); and Allan N. Schore, "The Experience-Dependent Maturation of a Regulatory System in the Orbital Prefrontal Cortex and the Origin of

Developmental Psychopathology," *Development and Psychopathology* 8 (1996): 59–87.

16. For a discussion on the psychological importance of names and the parent-child relationship, see Deborah Ann Luepnitz, *Schopenhauer's Porcupines: Intimacy and Its Dilemmas* (New York: Basic Books, 2002).

17. For more on the influence of sibling order on an individual, see Michael Lamb and Brian Sutton-Smith, eds., *Sibling Relationships: Their Nature and Significance Across the Lifespan* (Hillsdale, NJ: Lawrence Erlbaum, 1982).

18. Twenge, *Generation Me,* 3.

19. See Daniel Stern, *The Interpersonal World of the Infant* (New York: Basic Books, 1985), for a thorough discussion of the interpersonal processes that facilitate the many steps toward developing a sense of self.

20. For a discussion of Asian conceptualizations of the self that emphasize connection with others, see Hajime Nakamura, *Ways of Thinking of Eastern Peoples: India, China, Tibet, Japan* (London: Kegan Paul, 1964, 1999).

21. For a description of the stages of cognitive and intellectual development in children, see Jean Piaget and Barbel Inhelder, *The Psychology of the Child* (New York: Basic Books, 1969, 2000).

22. Throughout history, various societies have expected children to be capable of increased responsibility at the age of seven. For instance, court apprenticeships in the Middle Ages began at age seven, English common law held seven-year-olds legally accountable for their behavior, and currently the Catholic Church allows seven-year-olds to have their first communion. See Adele M. Brodkin, "Age of Reason," *Scholastic Parents,* July 1, 2006, www.content.scholastic.com.

23. For a discussion of the development of language and narratives, see Jerome Bruner, *Child's Talk: Learning to Use Language* (New York: W. W. Norton, 1983).

24. There are quite a few good books on the developmental importance of unstructured, child-led play. For example, see David Elkind, *The Power of Play: How Spontaneous, Imaginative Activities Lead to Happier, Healthier Children* (Cambridge, MA: Da Capo, 2007); Fergus P. Hughes, *Children, Play, and Development* (Needham Heights, MA: Allyn and Bacon, 1999); and Dorothy G.

Singer and Jerome L. Singer, *The House of Make-Believe: Children's Play and the Developing Imagination* (Cambridge, MA: Harvard University Press, 1990).

25. For a thorough summary of research findings on empathy development in children, see Kathleen Cotton, "Developing Empathy in Children and Youth," Northwest Regional Library, School Improvement Research Series, 1992, www.nwel.org/scpd/sirs/7/cu13.html.

Chapter Six: The Value of Being Ordinary

1. For a discussion of the recent trend toward promoting "giftedness" in children, see Quart, *Hothouse Kids*.

2. Dr. Marlene Maron is the director of Pediatric Psychological Services at Fletcher Allen Health Care, in Burlington, Vermont.

3. See Quart, *Hothouse Kids*.

4. In his overview of research on the correlates of happiness, David Myers summarizes studies that demonstrate a connection between close relationships and increased happiness. See David Myers, "The Funds, Friends, and Faith of Happy People," *American Psychologist* 55 (2000): 56–67.

5. See Daniel Goleman, Richard Boyatzis, and Annie McKee, *Primal Leadership: Learning to Lead by Emotional Intelligence* (Boston: Harvard Business School Press, 2004).

6. See Kristen Neff, "The Development and Validation of a Scale to Measure Self-Compassion," *Self and Identity* 2 (2003): 224–50.

7. See *A Nation Deceived: How Schools Hold Back America's Brightest Students,* vols. 1 and 2 (Iowa City: University of Iowa, 2004). Both volumes of this report are available online at www.nation deceived.org.

8. Ann Hulbert, "Can Genius Really Be Cultivated?," *New York Times Magazine,* November 20, 2005, 64–57.

9. Eric Konigsberg, "Prairie Fire: The Life and Death of a Prodigy," *New Yorker,* January 16, 2006, 44.

10. Ibid., 55.

11. For more about the positive effects of connecting with others and with a sense of common humanity, see Daniel Goleman, *Social Intelligence: The New Science of Human Relationships* (New York: Bantam, 2006), and Mark R. Leary et al., "Self-Compassion and Reactions to Unpleasant Self-Relevant Events: The Impli-

cations of Treating Oneself Kindly," *Journal of Personality and Social Psychology* 92 (2007): 887–904.

12. Schachter, "Andrew: Insecurity, Inferiority," 131–32.

13. See Michael Lewis, "Self-Conscious Emotions: Embarrassment, Pride, Shame, and Guilt," in *Handbook of Emotions,* 2nd ed., eds. Michael Lewis and Jeanette M. Haviland-Jones (New York: Guilford Press, 2000), 623–36.

14. For more information on primary emotions, see Paul Ekman, "Basic Emotions," in *Handbook of Cognition and Emotion,* eds. Tim Dalgleish and Mick Power (Sussex, UK: John Wiley and Sons, 1999), 45–60, and Robert Plutchik, "A General Psychoevolutionary Theory of Emotion," in *Emotion: Theory, Research, and Experience,* vol. 1 of *Theories of Emotion,* eds. Robert Plutchik and Henry Kellerman (New York: Academic Press, 1980), 3–33.

15. See Lewis, "Self-Conscious Emotions."

16. See Jerome Kagan, *The Second Year: The Emergence of Self-Awareness* (Cambridge, MA: Harvard University Press, 1981).

17. See Stern, *The Interpersonal World of the Infant,* for the interpersonal processes that facilitate the development of consensual reality. Also see Jerome Bruner, *Actual Minds, Possible Worlds* (Cambridge, MA: Harvard University Press, 1987), for a theoretical account of the interpersonal context of reality.

18. For more on the development of the superego, see Hans Blum, "Superego Formation"; Loewald, "Some Instinctual Manifestations of Superego Formation"; and Milrod, "The Superego."

19. For more on the importance of relationships in developing empathy, see Daniel Goleman's *Social Intelligence* and also his *Emotional Intelligence: Why It Can Matter More than IQ* (New York: Bantam, 1995).

20. For research on grandiosity and underlying feelings of inferiority, see Robert Raskin, Jill Novacek, and Robert Hogan, "Narcissism, Self-Esteem, and Defensive Self-Enhancement," *Journal of Personality* 59 (1991): 19–38; and David J. Schneider and David Turkat, "Self-Presentation Following Success or Failure: Defensive Self-Esteem Models," *Journal of Personality* 43 (1975): 127–35.

21. Such distortions can lead to the development of a "false self," in which an individual lacks a feeling of authenticity. See Susan Harter et al., "A Model of the Effects of Perceived Parent and Peer

Support on Adolescent False Self Behavior," *Child Development* 67 (1996): 360–74.

22. See Mihaly Csikszentmihalyi, *Flow: The Psychology of Optimal Experience* (New York: HarperCollins, 1990).

23. In Buddhism these practices are called the Six Paramitas. See Traleg Kyabgon, *The Essence of Buddhism: An Introduction to Its Philosophy and Practice* (Boston: Shambhala, 2001) for a description of these activities from a Buddhist perspective.

24. Hall, "The Older-and-Wiser Hypothesis."

Chapter Seven: Religion and Reverence

1. Since the 1950s overall church attendance has decreased by 30 percent, and the majority of that decrease has occurred since the 1980s. See Robert Putnam, *Bowling Alone* (New York: Simon & Schuster, 2000), 70–71.

2. Carl Jung, *Psychology and Religion* (New Haven, CT: Yale University Press, 1938), 5.

3. For example, see *The Secret*, DVD, directed by Drew Hariot (TS Production, LLC, 2006).

4. Shinzen Young has written and lectured extensively about Buddhism, Vipassana meditation, and pain management. He founded the Vipassana Support Institute, in Ontario, Canada, and travels around North America leading meditation retreats. For more information about Shinzen Young, see his Web site at www.shinzen .org.

5. Robert Thurman, trans., *The Tibetan Book of the Dead: Liberation Through Understanding in the Between* (New York: Bantam, 1994), 25.

6. See Robert Coles, *The Spiritual Life of Children* (Boston: Houghton Mifflin, 1990).

7. See Twenge, *Generation Me*, 108.

8. Patricia Leigh Brown, "In the Classroom, a New Focus on Quieting the Mind," *New York Times,* June 16, 2007, Education section.

Chapter Eight: Love and Its Near Enemy

1. Quoted in Otto Kernberg, *Love Relations: Normality and Pathology* (New Haven, CT: Yale University Press, 1995), 44.

2. Attachment theory was developed by John Bowlby, who asserted

that humans have a primary, instinctual need to develop close emotional relationships, and that these relationships are important for survival. See Bowlby, *Attachment;* John Bowlby, *Separation: Anxiety and Anger,* vol. 2 of *Attachment and Loss* (New York: Basic Books, 1973); and John Bowlby, *Loss: Sadness and Depression,* vol. 3 of *Attachment and Loss* (New York: Basic Books, 1980).

3. Bowlby discussed separation anxiety in his book *Attachment* and theorized that it helped promote survival by keeping infants close to their caregivers. Mary Ainsworth and her colleagues studied the process of separation and patterns of attachment between toddlers and caregivers; see Mary Ainsworth et al., *Patterns of Attachment: A Psychological Study of the Strange Situation* (Hillsdale, NJ: Lawrence Erlbaum, 1978).

4. For more on the process of grieving, for example, see Elizabeth Kubler-Ross and David Kessler, *On Grief and Grieving: Finding the Meaning of Grief Through the Five Stages of Loss* (New York: Scribner, 2005).

5. For more on the deep psychological bond between parent and infant, see Daniel Stern and Nadia Bruschweiler-Stern, *The Birth of a Mother: How the Motherhood Experience Changes You Forever* (New York: Basic Books, 1998), 125–28; Donald W. Winnicott, "Primary Maternal Preoccupation," in *Through Paediatrics to Psycho-Analysis: Collected Papers* (New York: Brunner-Routledge, 1992); and Donald W. Winnicott, *The Child and the Family: First Relationships* (London: Tavistock, 1969).

6. For more on the family dynamic of scapegoating, see Michael E. Kerr and Murray Bowen, *Family Evaluation: An Approach Based on Bowen Theory* (New York: W.W. Norton, 1988), and Murray Bowen, *Family Therapy in Clinical Practice* (New York: Jason Aronson, 1994).

7. See Suniya S. Luthar and Chris C. Sexton, "The High Price of Affluence," in *Advances in Child Development,* ed. Robert V. Kail (San Diego: Academic Press, 2005).

8. See, for example, Donald W. Winnicott, *The Maturational Processes and the Facilitating Environment* (New York: International Universities Press, 1965).

9. Nancy Mairs, *Ordinary Time: Cycles in Marriage, Faith, and Renewal* (Boston: Beacon Press, 1993).

10. Ibid., 144–45.
11. Ibid., 145.
12. Ibid., 146.
13. Ibid.
14. See New Strategist Editors, *Generation X: Americans Born 1965 to 1976,* 4th ed. (Ithaca, NY: New Strategist, 2004), 172. Also see Peter Gorner, "University of Chicago Sex Study Sees Love, Loneliness," *Chicago Tribune,* January 9, 2004. For U.S. statistics up to 2007, see the *Statistical Abstract of the United States,* U.S. Census Bureau, www.census.gov/compendia/statab.

Chapter Nine: The Truth About Happiness

1. Daniel Gilbert, *Stumbling on Happiness* (New York: Knopf, 2006), 20.
2. Ibid., 21.
3. Ibid., 153.
4. Ibid., 162.
5. *Sketches of Frank Gehry,* DVD, directed by Sydney Pollack (Culver City, CA: Sony Pictures Home Entertainment, 2006).
6. See, for example, Thomas D. Gilovich and Victoria H. Medvec, "The Experience of Regret: What, When, and Why." *Psychological Review* 102 (1995): 379–95.
7. Quoted in *Tricycle: The Buddhist Review,* Fall 2005: 77.
8. This speech practice is based on Right Speech, a Buddhist guideline for ethical conduct that is part of the Eightfold Path (eight guidelines for ending suffering). See Rob Nairn, *What Is Meditation?*

Bibliography

Ainsworth, Mary, Mary C. Blehar, Everett Waters, and Sally Wall. *Patterns of Attachment: A Psychological Study of the Strange Situation.* Hillsdale, NJ: Lawrence Erlbaum, 1978.

Ardelt, Monika. "Social Crisis and Individual Growth: The Long-term Effects of the Great Depression." *Journal of Aging Studies* 12 (1998): 291–314.

Arnett, Jeffrey J. *Emerging Adulthood: The Winding Road from the Late Teens to the Twenties.* New York: Oxford University Press, 2004.

Barber, Brian K., and Elizabeth L. Harmon. "Violating the Self: Parental Psychological Control of Children and Adolescents." In *Intrusive Parenting: How Psychological Control Affects Children and Adolescents,* edited by Brian K. Barber. Washington, DC: American Psychological Association, 2002.

Baumrind, Diana. "Rearing Competent Children." In *Child Development Today and Tomorrow,* edited by William Damon. San Francisco: Jossey-Bass, 1989.

Bellah, Robert, Richard Madsen, William M. Sullivan, Ann Swidler, and Steven M. Tipton. *Habits of the Heart: Individualism and Commitment in American Life.* New York: Harper and Row, 1985.

Blum, Hans. "Superego Formation, Adolescent Transformation, and Adult Neurosis." *Journal of the Psychoanalytic Association* 33 (1985): 887–910.

Bowen, Murray. *Family Therapy in Clinical Practice.* New York: Jason Aronson, 1994.

Bowlby, John. *Attachment.* Vol. 1, *Attachment and Loss.* New York: Basic Books, 1969.

———. *Loss: Sadness and Depression.* Vol. 3, *Attachment and Loss.* New York: Basic Books, 1980.

———. *Separation: Anxiety and Anger.* Vol. 2, *Attachment and Loss.* New York: Basic Books, 1973.

Brodkin, Adele M. "Age of Reason." *Scholastic Parents,* July 1, 2006, www.content.scholastic.com.

Brown, Patricia Leigh. "In the Classroom, a New Focus on Quieting the Mind." *New York Times,* June 16, 2007, Education section.

Brumberg, Joan J. "Are We Facing an Epidemic of Self-Injury?" *Chronicle of Higher Education* 53 (2006): B6.

Bruner, Jerome. *Actual Minds, Possible Words.* Cambridge, MA: Harvard University Press, 1987.

———. *Child's Talk: Learning to Use Language.* New York: W. W. Norton, 1983.

Burhans, Karen K., and Carol S. Dweck. "Helplessness in Early Childhood: The Role of Contingent Worth." *Child Development* 66 (1995): 1719–38.

Carroll, Lee, and Jan Tober. *The Indigo Children: The New Kids Have Arrived.* Carlsbad, CA: Light Technology Publications, 1999.

Coles, Robert. *The Spiritual Life of Children.* Boston: Houghton Mifflin, 1990.

Columbia World of Quotations. Edited by Robert Andrews, Mary Briggs, and Michael Seidel. New York: Columbia University Press, 1996. www.bartleby.com/66/78/38578.html.

Cotton, Kathleen. "Developing Empathy in Children and Youth." Northwest Regional Library, School Improvement Research Series, 1992. www.nwel.org/scpd/sirs/7/cu13.html.

Csikszentmihalyi, Mihaly. *Flow: The Psychology of Optimal Experience.* New York: HarperCollins, 1990.

Dalai Lama. *The Four Noble Truths.* London: Thorsons, 1997.

Diagnostic and Statistical Manual of Mental Disorders, 4th Edition, Text Revision (DSM-IV-TR). Edited by Michael B. First. Washington, DC: American Psychiatric Publishing, 2000.

"Do Ethics Still Matter?: Lichtman/Zobgy Poll of Young Americans Say 'Yes, But . . . .' " Zogby International, May 9, 2005. www.zogby.com/news/ReadNews.dbm?ID=991.

Eisenstock, Alan. *The Kindergarten Wars: The Battle to Get Into America's Best Private Schools.* New York: Warner, 2006.

Ekman, Paul. "Basic Emotions." In *Handbook of Cognition and Emotion,* edited by Tim Dalgleish and Mick Power. Sussex, UK: John Wiley and Sons, 1999.

Elkind, David. "Egocentrism in Adolescence." In *Readings in Developmental Psychology,* 2nd ed., edited by Judith Krieger Gardner and Ed Gardner. Reading, MA: Addison-Wesley, 1978.

———. *The Power of Play: How Spontaneous, Imaginative Activities Lead to Happier, Healthier Children.* Cambridge, MA: Da Capo, 2007.

Ephraim, David. "A Psychocultural Approach to TAT Scoring." In *Handbook of Cross-cultural and Multicultural Personality Assessment,* edited by R. H. Dana. Mahwaw, NJ: Lawrence Erlbaum, 2000.

Epstein, Mark. *Going to Pieces Without Falling Apart: A Buddhist Perspective on Wholeness.* New York: Broadway Books, 1998.

Erikson, Erik. *Childhood and Society.* New York: W. W. Norton, 1964, 1986, 1993.

Farkas, Steve, and Jean Johnson, with Ann Duffett and Kathleen Collins. "Aggravating Circumstances: A Status Report on Rudeness in America." Public Agenda, 2002. www.publicagenda.org/research/research-reports-details.cfm?list=19.

Feldman, S. Shirley, and Elizabeth Cauffman. "Sexual Betrayal Among Late Adolescents: Perspectives of the Perpetrator and the Aggrieved." *Journal of Youth and Adolescence* 28 (1999): 235–58.

Foster, Joshua, Keith Campbell, and Jean Twenge. "Individual Differences in Narcissism: Inflated Self-Views Across the Lifespan and Around the World." *Journal of Research in Personality* 37 (2002): 469–86.

Fulton, Paul R., and Ronald D. Siegel. "Buddhist and Western Psychology: Seeking Common Ground." In *Mindfulness and Psychotherapy,* edited by C. K. Germer, R. D. Siegel, and P. R. Fulton. New York: Guilford Press, 2005.

Garber, Judy B., N. S. Robinson, and D. Valentiner. "The Relationship Between Parenting Style and Adolescent Depression: Self-Worth as a Mediator." *Journal of Adolescent Research* 12 (1997): 12–33.

Gilbert, Daniel. *Stumbling on Happiness.* New York: Knopf, 2006.

Gilovich, Thomas D., and Victoria H. Medvec. "The Experience of Regret: What, When, and Why." *Psychological Review* 102 (1995): 379–95.

Glatter, Jonathan D. "To: Professor@University.edu; Subject: Why It's All About Me." *New York Times,* February 12, 2006, Education section.

Goff, Karen G. "Lessons in Life: Sharing Space; Rules Help as Children Compromise." *Washington Times,* October 10, 2004, section D.

Goleman, Daniel. *Emotional Intelligence: Why It Can Matter More than IQ*. New York: Bantam, 1995.

————. *Social Intelligence: The New Science of Human Relationships*. New York: Bantam, 2006.

Goleman, Daniel, Richard Boyatzis, and Annie McKee. *Primal Leadership: Learning to Lead by Emotional Intelligence*. Boston: Harvard Business School Press, 2004.

Goodall, Jane. *The Chimpanzees of Gombe: Patterns of Behavior*. Boston: Harvard University Press, 1986.

Gorner, Peter. "University of Chicago Sex Study Sees Love, Loneliness." *Chicago Tribune,* January 9, 2004.

Gottman, John. *Raising an Emotionally Intelligent Child: The Heart of Parenting*. New York: Fireside, 1997.

Greenough, William T., and James E. Black. "Induction of Brain Structure by Experience: Substrates for Cognitive Development." In *Minnesota Symposia on Child Psychology: Developmental Neuroscience,* vol. 24, edited by M. R. Gunnar and C. A. Nelson. Hillsdale, NJ: Lawrence Erlbaum, 1997.

Grello, Catherine M., Deborah P. Welsh, and Melinda S. Harper. "No Strings Attached: The Nature of Casual Sex in College Students." *Journal of Sex Research* 43 (2006): 255–67.

Habito, Ruben L. F. *Experiencing Buddhism: Ways of Wisdom and Compassion*. Maryknoll, NY: Orbis Books, 2005.

Hackney, Suzette. "More Adult Children Returning to the Nest: It's a Cultural Custom for Some and a Financial Need for Others." *Houston Chronicle,* June 19, 2006, Business section.

Hall, Stephen S. "The Older-and-Wiser Hypothesis." *New York Times Magazine,* May 6, 2007.

Harré, Rom. *Personal Being: A Theory for Individual Psychology*. Cambridge, MA: Harvard University Press, 1986.

Harris, Thomas A. *I'm OK—You're OK: A Practical Guide to Transactional Analysis*. New York: Harper and Row, 1969.

Harter, Susan, Donna Marold, Nancy Whitesell, and Gabrielle Cobbs. "A Model of the Effects of Perceived Parent and Peer Support on Adolescent False Self Behavior." *Child Development* 67 (1996): 360–74.

Hewitt, John. *The Myth of Self-Esteem: Finding Happiness and Solving Problems in America*. New York: St. Martin's, 1998.

Hightower, Elaine, and Betsy Riley. *Our Family Meeting Book: Fun and Easy Ways to Manage Time, Build Communication, and Share Responsibility Week by Week*. Minneapolis: Free Spirit, 2002.

Hilfiker, David. *Healing the Wounds: A Doctor Looks at His Work.* New York: Pantheon, 1985.

———. *Not All of Us Are Saints: A Doctor's Journey with the Poor.* New York: Ballantine, 1994.

Hilfiker, Karin. "Tears of Grief, Tears of Joy." *With,* December 1991.

Hughes, Fergus P. *Children, Play, and Development.* Needham Heights, MA: Allyn and Bacon, 1999.

Hulbert, Ann. "Can Genius Really Be Cultivated?" *New York Times Magazine,* November 20, 2005.

Irvine, Martha. "Age of 'Entitlement' Changes Rules: Generation of Workers Demand More from Workplace." *Grand Rapids Press,* July 3, 2005, section H.

———. "Young Labeled 'Entitlement Generation.'" Associated Press, June 26, 2005. www.bizyahoo.com/ap/050626/the_entitlement_generation.html 2.v3.

Josephson Institute of Ethics. "2004 Josephson Institute Report Card on Ethics of American Youth: Part One—Integrity." www.josephson institute.org/Survey2004/2004reportcard-pressrelease.htm.

Jung, Carl. *Psychology and Religion.* New Haven, CT: Yale University Press, 1938.

Kagan, Jerome. *The Second Year: The Emergence of Self-Awareness.* Cambridge, MA: Harvard University Press, 1981.

Kantrowitz, Barbara, and Peg Tyre. "The Fine Art of Letting Go." *Newsweek,* May 22, 2006.

Kegan, Robert. *The Evolving Self: Problem and Process in Human Development.* Cambridge, MA: Harvard University Press, 1982.

Kellogg, Alex P. "Facing More, and Possibly Pickier Students, Colleges Renovate and Add Housing." *Chronicle of Higher Education,* October 19, 2001.

Kernberg, Otto. *Love Relations: Normality and Pathology.* New Haven, CT: Yale University Press, 1995.

Kerr, Michael E., and Murray Bowen. *Family Evaluation: An Approach Based on Bowen Theory.* New York: W.W. Norton, 1988.

Kindlon, Dan. *Too Much of a Good Thing: Raising Children of Character in an Indulgent Age.* New York: Mirimax, 2001.

Kohn, Alfie. *Unconditional Parenting: Moving from Rewards and Punishments to Love and Reason.* New York: Atria Books, 2005.

Konigsberg, Eric. "Prairie Fire: The Life and Death of a Prodigy." *New Yorker,* January 16, 2006.

Kramer, D. A. "Wisdom as a Classical Source of Human Strength: Conceptualization and Empirical Inquiry." *Journal of Social and Clinical Psychology* 19 (2000): 83–101.

Kubler-Ross, Elizabeth, and David Kessler. *On Grief and Grieving: Finding the Meaning of Grief Through the Five Stages of Loss.* New York: Scribner, 2005.

Kyabgon, Traleg. *The Essence of Buddhism: An Introduction to Its Philosophy and Practice.* Boston: Shambhala, 2001.

Lamb, Michael, and Brian Sutton-Smith, eds. *Sibling Relationships: Their Nature and Significance Across the Lifespan.* Hillsdale, NJ: Lawrence Erlbaum, 1982.

Lamb, Sharon, and Lyn Mikel Brown. *Packaging Girlhood: Rescuing Our Daughters from Marketers' Schemes.* New York: St. Martin's, 2006.

Lareau, Annette. *Unequal Childhoods: Class, Race, and Family Life.* Berkeley: University of California Press, 2003.

Lasch, Christopher. *The Culture of Narcissism.* New York: W. W. Norton, 1979.

Leary, Mark R., Eleanor B. Tate, Claire E. Adams, Ashley B. Allen, and Jessica Hancock. "Self-Compassion and Reactions to Unpleasant Self-Relevant Events: The Implications of Treating Oneself Kindly." *Journal of Personality and Social Psychology* 92 (2007): 887–904.

LeDoux, Joseph. *The Synaptic Self: How Our Brains Become Who We Are.* New York: Viking, 2002.

Lehr, Dick, and Mitchell Zuckoff. *Judgment Ridge: The True Story Behind the Dartmouth Murders.* New York: HarperCollins, 2003.

Leland, John. "Are They Here to Save the World?" *New York Times,* January 12, 2006, Health section.

Levine, Madeline. *The Price of Privilege: How Parental Pressure and Material Advantage Are Creating a Generation of Disconnected and Unhappy Kids.* New York: HarperCollins, 2006.

Lewinsohn, Peter M., Paul Rohde, John Seeley, and Stanley Fischer. "Age-Cohort Changes in the Lifetime Occurrence of Depression and Other Mental Disorders." *Journal of Abnormal Psychology* 102 (1993): 110–20.

Lewis, Michael. "Self-Conscious Emotions: Embarrassment, Pride, Shame, and Guilt." In *Handbook of Emotions,* 2nd ed., edited by Michael Lewis and Jeanette M. Haviland-Jones. New York: Guilford Press, 2000.

Lewontin, Richard C. *Biology and Ideology: The Doctrine of DNA.* Toronto: House of Anansi Press, 1991.

Loewald, Hans W. "Some Instinctual Manifestations of Superego Formation." *Annual of Psychoanalysis* 1 (1973): 104–16.

Luepnitz, Deborah Ann. *Schopenhauer's Porcupines: Intimacy and Its Dilemmas.* New York: Basic Books, 2002.

Luthar, Suniya S., and Chris C. Sexton. "The High Price of Affluence." In *Advances in Child Development,* edited by Robert V. Kail. San Diego: Academic Press, 2005.

Mairs, Nancy. *Ordinary Time: Cycles in Marriage, Faith, and Renewal.* Boston: Beacon Press, 1993.

Maurer, Harry. "Enron: Guilty, Guilty, Guilty." *Business Week,* June 12, 2006.

Mellor, Christie. *The Three-Martini Playdate: A Practical Guide to Happy Parenting.* San Francisco: Chronicle, 2004.

Miller, Alice. *The Drama of the Gifted Child: The Search for the True Self.* New York: HarperCollins, 1996.

Milrod, David. "The Superego: Its Formation, Structure, and Functioning." *Psychoanalytic Study of the Child* 57 (2002): 131–48.

Mitchell, Stephen A., and Margaret J. Black. *Freud and Beyond: A History of Modern Psychoanalytic Thought.* New York: Basic Books, 1995.

Myers, David. "The Funds, Friends, and Faith of Happy People." *American Psychologist* 55 (2000): 56–67.

Nagapriya. *Exploring Karma and Rebirth.* Birmingham, UK: Windhorse, 2005.

Nairn, Rob. *What Is Meditation?: Buddhism for Everyone.* Boston: Shambhala, 2000.

Nakamura, Hajime. *Ways of Thinking of Eastern Peoples: India, China, Tibet, Japan.* London: Kegan Paul, 1964, 1999.

National Institutes of Health, National Institute of Mental Health. *Teenage Brain: A Work in Progress.* NIH Publication No. 01-4929, 2001.

A Nation Deceived: How Schools Hold Back America's Brightest Students. 2 vols. Iowa City: University of Iowa, 2004. www.nationdeceived.org.

Neff, Kristen. "The Development and Validation of a Scale to Measure Self-Compassion." *Self and Identity* 2 (2003): 224–50.

Neff, Kristen, Ya-Ping Hsieh, and Kullaya Dejitterat. "Self-Compassion, Achievement Goals, and Coping with Academic Failure." *Self and Identity* 2 (2005): 263–87.

Newson, C. R. "Changes in Adolescent Response Patterns on the MMPI/ MMPI-A Across Four Decades." *Journal of Personality Assessment* 81 (2003): 74–84.

New Strategist Editors. *Generation X: Americans Born 1965 to 1976.* 4th ed. Ithaca, NY: New Strategist, 2004.

O'Leary, Virginia E., and Jeanette R. Ickovics. "Resilience and Thriving in Response to Challenge: An Opportunity for a Paradigm Shift in Women's Health." *Women's Health: Research on Gender, Behavior, and Policy* 1 (1995): 121–42.

Peterson, Christopher, and Martin E. P. Seligman. *Character Strengths and Virtues: A Handbook and Classification.* New York: American Psychological Association and Oxford University Press, 2004.

Piaget, Jean. *The Moral Judgment of the Child.* New York: Free Press Paperbacks, 1997.

Piaget, Jean, and Barbel Inhelder. *The Psychology of the Child.* New York: Basic Books, 1969, 2000.

Plutchik, Robert. "A General Psychoevolutionary Theory of Emotion." In *Emotion: Theory, Research, and Experience.* Vol. 1, *Theories of Emotion.* Edited by Robert Plutchik and Henry Kellerman. New York: Academic Press, 1980.

Pollack, William. *Real Boys: Rescuing Our Sons from the Myths of Boyhood.* New York: Owl Books, 1999.

Putnam, Robert. *Bowling Alone.* New York: Simon & Schuster, 2000.

Quart, Alissa. *Hothouse Kids: The Dilemma of the Gifted Child.* New York: Penguin, 2006.

Raskin, Robert, Jill Novacek, and Robert Hogan. "Narcissism, Self-Esteem, and Defensive Self-Enhancement." *Journal of Personality* 59 (1991): 19–38.

Robbins, Alexandra. *The Overachievers: The Secret Lives of Driven Kids.* New York: Hyperion, 2006.

Rosemond, John K. "The Diseasing of America's Children: The Politics of Diagnosis." In *Destructive Trends in Mental Health: The Well-Intentioned Path to Harm,* edited by R. H. Wright and N. A. Cummings. New York: Routledge, 2005.

Rutter, Michael. "Psychosocial Resilience and Proactive Mechanisms." *American Journal of Orthopsychiatry* 57 (1987): 316–31.

Schachter, Joseph. "Andrew: Insecurity, Inferiority, Social Anxiety, and Submissiveness." In *Transforming Lives: Analyst and Patient View the Power of Psychoanalytic Treatment,* edited by Joseph Schachter. New York: Jason Aronson, 2005.

Schneider, David J., and David Turkat. "Self-Presentation Following Success or Failure: Defensive Self-Esteem Models." *Journal of Personality* 43 (1975): 127–35.

Schore, Allan N. "The Experience-Dependent Maturation of a Regulatory System in the Orbital Prefrontal Cortex and the Origin of Developmental Psychopathology." *Development and Psychopathology* 8 (1996): 59–87.

The Secret, DVD. Directed by Drew Hariot. N.p., TS Production, LLC, 2006.

Singer, Dorothy G., and Jerome L. Singer. *The House of Make-Believe: Children's Play and the Developing Imagination.* Cambridge, MA: Harvard University Press, 1990.

Sketches of Frank Gehry, DVD. Directed by Sydney Pollack. Culver City, CA: Sony Pictures Home Entertainment, 2006.

Sowell, Elizabeth R., Paul M. Thompson, Colin J. Holmes, Terry L. Jernigan, and Arthur W. Toga. "In Vivo Evidence for Post-Adolescent Brain Maturation in Frontal and Striatal Regions." *Nature Neuroscience* 2 (1999): 859–61.

Statistical Abstract of the United States. U.S. Census Bureau. www.census .gov/compendia/statab.

Stern, Daniel. *The Interpersonal World of the Infant.* New York: Basic Books, 1985.

Stern, Daniel, and Nadia Bruschweiler-Stern. *The Birth of a Mother: How the Motherhood Experience Changes You Forever.* New York: Basic Books, 1998.

Taylor, Charles. *The Sources of the Self: The Making of Modern Identity.* Cambridge, MA: Harvard University Press, 1989.

Thurman, Robert, trans. *The Tibetan Book of the Dead: Liberation Through Understanding in the Between.* New York: Bantam, 1994.

Tugade, Michele M., and Barbara L. Fredrickson. "Resilient Individuals Use Positive Emotions to Bounce Back from Negative Emotional Experiences." *Journal of Personality and Social Psychology* 86 (2004): 320–33.

Twenge, Jean M. *Generation Me: Why Today's Young Americans Are More Confident, Assertive, Entitled—and More Miserable Than Ever Before.* New York: Free Press, 2006.

U.S. Department of Health and Human Services. "2005 Survey on Drug Use and Health: National Results." Office of Applied Studies, SAMHSA. www.oas.samhsa.gov/NSDUH/2k5NSDUH/2k5results.htm#Ch3.

Vandehei, Jim. "Probe Focuses on Rove's Testimony; As He Wraps Up, Special Counsel Asking if Deputy Chief of Staff Lied About Conversation." *Houston Chronicle,* May 8, 2006.

Warner, Judith. "Kids Gone Wild." *New York Times,* November 27, 2005, Week in Review section.

————. *Perfect Madness: Motherhood in the Age of Anxiety.* New York: Riverhead Books, 2005.

Watson, P. J., Tracy Little, and Michael D. Biderman. "Narcissism and Parenting Styles." *Psychoanalytic Psychology* 9 (1992): 231–44.

Webster's II New College Dictionary. 2nd ed. Boston: Houghton Mifflin, 1999.

Wickramaratne, Priya J., Myrna M. Weissman, Philip J. Leaf, and Theodore R. Holford. "Age, Period, and Cohort Effects on the Risk of Major Depression: Results from Five United States Communities." *Journal of Clinical Epidemiology* 42 (1989): 333–43.

Winnicott, Donald W. *The Child and the Family: First Relationships.* London: Tavistock, 1969.

————. *The Maturational Processes and the Facilitating Environment.* New York: International Universities Press, 1965.

————. "Primary Maternal Preoccupation." In *Through Paediatrics to Psycho-Analysis: Collected Papers.* New York: Brunner-Routledge, 1992.

Young-Eisendrath, Polly. *Gender and Desire: Uncursing Pandora.* College Station: Texas A&M University Press, 1997.

————. *Women and Desire: Beyond Wanting to Be Wanted.* New York: Three Rivers Press, 1999.

————. *You're Not What I Expected: Learning to Love the Opposite Sex.* New York: William Morrow, 1993.

Young-Eisendrath, Polly, and Terence Dawson, eds. *The Cambridge Companion to Jung.* Cambridge, England: Cambridge University Press, 1997.

Young-Eisendrath, Polly, and James Hall. *Jung's Self Psychology: A Constructivist Perspective.* New York: Guilford Press, 1991.

Young-Eisendrath, Polly, and Florence Wiedemann. *Female Authority: Empowering Women Through Psychotherapy.* New York: Guilford Press, 1987.

Zito, Julie M., Daniel J. Safer, Susan DosReis, James F. Gardner, Laurence Magder, Karen Soeken, Myde Boles, Frances Lynch, and Mark A. Riddle. "Psychotropic Practice Patterns for Youth: A Ten-Year Perspective." *Archives of Pediatrics and Adolescent Medicine* 157 (2003): 17–25.

Zolten, Kristen, and Nicholas Long. "Family Meetings." Center for Effective Parenting, Arkansas State PIRC, 1997. www.parenting-ed.org/parenting-handouts.htm.

Index